To Gill, Connie & Gill

Best wishes.

Pat howther

Oct. 2007.

VINTAGE 1930

VINTAGE 1930

Story of a Twentieth-Century Woman

Patricia M. Lowther

Book Guild Publishing
Sussex, England

First published in Great Britain in 2007 by
The Book Guild Ltd
Pavilion View
19 New Road
Brighton BN1 1UF

Typesetting in Times by
Keyboard Services, Luton, Bedfordshire

Printed in Great Britain by
CPI Antony Rowe

A catalogue record for this book is available from
The British Library

ISBN 978 1 84624 135 2

1

Some years ago when we lived in Croydon I was a member of the local Townswomen's Guild. Within it we had a smaller section who met in members' homes once a month where we would take turns to present a paper on the selected topic for the year. One year the topic was 'My Life' and each one in turn told us her life story and what her family background had been. They were many and varied. The family of one had owned a well-established butcher's business with shops all around the south of London. Another came from the East End of London and as a child would go to the hop fields every year. But almost invariably their lives seemed to go on hold with the final sentence, where they explained that they met and married their husbands and had a family. Well, I suppose for my generation this was probably the norm, but it certainly didn't happen like that for me!

I have not been in the habit of keeping a diary although from time to time I have tried. Some three or four years ago, reading what I had written, I couldn't help thinking how boring it was, just a list of the things I had done from day to day. I suppose the essence of attempting to write about your life is that you must stand back from its events and with the aid of hindsight show the big picture and skate around all the boring minutiae.

I was born at home on 15 July 1930 at 4a, Warwick Street, Heaton in Newcastle, the first and, as it transpired, the only child of my parents, Bill and Maud Trobe. Bill was the middle son in a family of three sons and three daughters. Grandfather was a jeweller and watchmaker and he and my

1

grandmother lived at Victoria House on Heaton Park Road. My parents' home was the upstairs flat of a converted house nearby. My father and his younger brother, Stan, had set up business together as builders' merchants and they owned several trucks which would convey the building materials to the various sites. My mother was the youngest of three sisters; the others were Elsie, the eldest, and May, each a year apart. Her mother, Grandma Wilson, had been the child of Irish immigrants living in Jarrow and as a thirteen-year-old she was sent to live and work in a pub on the quayside in Newcastle. To begin with she looked after the publican's children and I remember her telling me her duties included banking up the coal fire at night and then filling up the large pot with water and porridge oats and setting it at the back of the fire so that the children's breakfast would be ready first thing in the morning. She wasn't very tall so I dare say there wasn't much difference in size between herself and the children. When she was old enough she worked in the pub where the customs officers employed on the quayside would call in for their lunchtime pint. At that time there was a lot of shipping in the Tyne and there were sizeable customs sheds where goods attracting excise duty were held. Here she caught the eye of my grandfather, Alfred Wilson, and when the publican realised she was pregnant, he suggested he do the decent thing. My grandmother, Bridget Coyne, good Irish girl that she was, found that her new husband would have nothing to do with her church. He came from Yorkshire stock, so I was told, and his family disowned him on his marriage. She went on to have a child every year; the eldest was a boy, Arthur, then came Elsie and May and finally my mother. When my mother was two weeks old, both Arthur and my grandfather died of pneumonia. The customs authorities offered to take the children to be brought up in one of their homes, but Grandma refused and instead took them all off to the nearest Catholic church to be baptised.

This final insult led to a complete split with her husband's family and she never saw them again.

There were no pensions in those days so the neighbours looked after the little girls while she did cleaning in people's homes or took their washing to the public wash-house. May used to tell me that as they came home from school they would call down to their mother through the windows that lay at ground level as she did the washing. I have a photo of her, however, at the one time when she probably had a bit of money. She is wearing the overall and cap of a munitions worker during the First World War. There is also a battered old photo of Grandfather in his customs officer's uniform.

The family lived at 86, Oban Road, Byker, which later became a notorious slum and is probably no longer there now.

So for Maudie to meet and marry a young man with his own business and their own house (notwithstanding the mortgage payments!) must have seemed a miracle. Apparently when I was born Grandma Wilson held me in her arms and said: 'This child is born with a silver spoon in her mouth.' To her, after the privation she had experienced, it must have certainly seemed so.

At weekends my parents and my uncles and aunts would go out in the car for picnics into the countryside or down to the coast. My father preferred the countryside as he said he hated sand in his sandwiches. I have an old black-and-white photo which my daughter Anne had enlarged for me showing the young couple lying on the grass with me at about eight or nine months old, gazing proudly at their child. It was not to last. Before long Maudie's cough became worse and it was evident that the trials of her childhood had caught up with her. She was suffering from tuberculosis. There followed long periods of time in the sanatorium at Barrasford, a word that haunted my childhood, and which must have strained their finances in the days before free medical care. I still have a packet of letters that May gave me – letters my mother wrote to her from Barrasford, full of optimism and expectant of a cure, but it was not to be.

My grandfather had bought a house at the bottom of Benton Bank which had been a farmhouse. I remember going there when I was four and seeing the big farm gate and the piggery at the back. On the land next to it my father and Uncle Stan built a pair of semi-detached houses and I still have a list my mother made of features for the house, plus all the final bills for the construction. I was about five when we moved in, but it was there that my mother died at the age of 29 on 12 January 1936.

I still remember that day. I had been in our house with my parents. A bed had been set up for my mother in the dining room at the back of the house looking out through the French doors into the back garden where her garden swing had been during the preceding summer. My father asked me to go next door to my grandmother's house and I went out of the back door and down the small flight of concrete steps that had been made to give access between the two houses. (Later, when the house was let during the war, they were filled in, but no doubt they still exist under the earth.) In my grandmother's house she and my father's two unmarried sisters, Maryon and Ethel – casualties of the First World War which decimated the male population – were seated around the fire where one roasted in front and froze at the rear as the drafts swept in under the doors. Maryon always sat with legs spread wide and one foot inside the hearth, and consequently her veins were outlined on her legs where the heat had toasted them. We sat together; no one asked me why I was there – I expect they knew. Then my father came in to the room and asked me to come into the drawing room with him. There he gently told me that my mother was dead. I do not know if I really realised what this meant or that I would never see her again. In truth she was rather a wraithlike shape in my life with her intermittent absences at Barrasford, and I do not recall having much physical contact with her; no doubt she was warned not to embrace me because of the risk of infection. But it was a turning point and the fact that I remember it so well must surely mean that I was aware that things had changed.

I don't remember feeling any personal grief, but from then on there was a void in my life, the fabric of our family had been rent and where certainty had been, there was a yawning gap which was never to be filled. In my old age I can look back and appreciate what a loss a mother's death is; there is no one who will fight your corner, back you up, praise and protect you. You are isolated and as the years pass you learn nothing of the art of motherhood so that when you become a mother yourself, you have no signposts to follow.

I did not go to my mother's funeral; I was sent to school while it took place and I have been told that when I came home and saw all the people in the house I asked why we were having a party. The problem for my father now was who would care for me. I believe he asked my mother's favourite sister, May, if she and her husband, Alfie, and their son, David, would move into his house with him, but needless to say, Alfie refused. My grandparents' house was full with them and my two aunts, so eventually Florence came to live with us. It was quite usual in those days to have a maid and Florence had the small box room over the front door, my father had the main bedroom and my room was at the back looking out over the garden and into the park beyond. I loved Florence – she had a limp, she was rather plain but she cared for me and looked after our house and, I suspect, harboured unrequited feelings for my father. So our lives settled down. I used to walk to school; to begin with it was to a little wooden building, but later a brand new school was built a little further away, called Cragside Junior School.

5

Looking at the path I took I am amazed that small children happily made their way along busy roads and over well-used junctions without any fear. Once I fell down and grazed my knee and a little school friend insisted on taking me home to her mother. They lived in a council house on the estate which I walked past every day and her mother took me in, bathed my knee and put iodine on it. I was sent off home with a piece of bread and jam and I envied that little girl her crowded loving home.

My father's elder brother was also a haulage contractor and builders' merchant. His lorries were painted red and he had HENRY TROBE printed on the front. My father and his brother, Stan, had yellow lorries and the business was called Trobe Bros. Ltd. So for me, the old tongue twister of 'red lorries, yellow lorries' had real significance. Harry was a real go-getter and his business prospered. He teamed up with a local builder and they brought timber over to the Tyne from the Scandinavian countries ... possibly Norway ... and sold it on at a good profit. He met my aunt, Nancy when she was separated from her husband and had a daughter called Joyce. In those days divorce was either for adultery or desertion and it seems there were difficulties, so Harry arranged some under-the-counter deal, the details of which I am not aware, but it was discovered so there was no divorce. My cousin Marian was four months older than me and it wasn't until many years later that I learned the truth. Her brother Harry was three or four years younger. When we had all grown up, apparently the opportunity arose for their position to be legalised, but Nancy had to fight long and hard to get him to the altar. Uncle Harry had been just old enough to be in the Flying Corps towards the end of the First World War. He was a short man with explosive energy who embraced the passion of the moment, skiing, caravanning, pistol shooting, yachting, with great enthusiasm. He became the commodore at the Tynemouth Yacht Club and although he always had a white Jaguar he

6

would expect my aunt to go to the annual dinner dance in his beat-up old Mini.

My father was of a quieter disposition and he and Stan got on well. Sadly Stan also died of tuberculosis and his widow, also called Nancy, insisted on cashing in her share of the business. He never really recovered financially from that.

Of my father's three sisters, Maryon was the eldest child. She was quite a noted dog breeder in the area; starting with sealyams, she changed to spaniels and brought one of the first cocker spaniels to England from America. His name was Tommy and one day Uncle Harry took him to the airfield where the local flying club gathered. He ran off and was killed on the electric rail line while trying to make his way home. I spent many hours at dog shows with her and learned how to 'show' a dog at an early age. It was not unusual to go to my grandmother's and find a litter of puppies keeping warm in the hearth. Later she changed to corgis and one of the last dogs we had was one of the pups she bred.

My greatest friend, however, was Ross. He was a very large Alsatian who had belonged to a friend of Auntie Ethel who had gone to Australia and left him with his parents. They had him tied up in their back yard and were frightened of him, so he came to us, and although he was supposed to be Ethel's dog, in reality he was mine and took the place of siblings from when I was five until I was fifteen.

Gladys, also known as Dolly, was the youngest child and I think somewhat spoilt. In the late 1930s she and Ethel went for a holiday to Bassenthwaite in the Lake District and at the local Saturday night dance she met Isaac Thwaites, who lived with his father and his two sisters on a farm on the slopes of Skiddaw. He was due to emigrate to Australia as well and on his way through Newcastle he called on my grandfather to ask for Dolly's hand in marriage. So Dolly sailed to Australia where she and Isaac were duly married and ran a fruit farm. During the war years life was often improved by a food parcel containing raisins and sultanas among other things.

My maternal aunts, Elsie and May, figured largely in my life. Especially being at their houses on a Monday where they took turns for my Grandmother Wilson to come and help them on wash day. This involved clothes being boiled in the gas boiler, blued and starched in the tin bath and hung out in the back lane until such time as the coal man came along with his truck. At the first cry of 'Coal!' there would be a concerted rush up and down the lane as all the housewives took their washing in.

May was married to Alfie and was the next to marry after my mother. My parents were married in the Church of England church on Heaton Road, as I was, years later. May however, was married in the Catholic Church in Byker, but only at a side altar as Alfie was not a Catholic. He was the only son of his parents, who ran a little corner shop in Byker. I loved going to Grandpa and Grandma Cleminson, as they would take the little metal hammer and break me off a piece of toffee from the tin tray that lay on the counter. They did a brisk trade in what was known as Parrishes checks. These were a form of credit that could be had on tick at the local department store and repaid at so much a week. When money was short the hard-up customers would sell them for cash to the little shop and May and Elsie would go off to Parrishes to spend the checks. I asked my father about the realities of these transactions once and when he explained, I could not understand how people could be so short sighted as to be forever in debt. But now I understand that these were desperate women with families to feed and husbands who probably drank their wages before they could reach their hard-pressed families.

Elsie, although the eldest, was the last to marry, and it smacked of desperation. Uncle Bob was a weedy little man who was a merchant seaman and away for long periods of time. So when Elsie became pregnant, she said he had come home unexpectedly without anyone knowing. I remember her son being born; we went to the hospital to bring them home and I had to wait outside. A passing nurse asked me if I was waiting for my new brother, it seemed too much trouble to explain, so I said 'yes' and thus told my first social lie! Bob said she would never have a child by him, and she didn't, but her son was the complete antithesis of her husband, handsome and robust. About this time I remember hearing my Aunt Ethel saying that it is a wise child who knows its own father. I was quite puzzled and challenged her, saying of course I knew who my father was. Muttering something about 'little pitchers' she changed the subject, but when years later I learned what had happened, that conversation came to mind and I wondered if Elsie had been the subject.

So life on my father's side was what you might call middle class, where everyone owned their own homes and had cars at a time when they were still scarce, while on my mother's side they lived well but within the communities where poverty was not far away.

After Uncle Stan died, my Grandfather Trobe also died.

One day in August 1939, my father asked me if I would like to go and live in the country. As we had many excursions and family holidays into the beautiful county of Northumberland, this idea quite appealed to me. I had a very firm idea of what it would be like. There would be a pretty stone cottage and a stream running through a meadow where I could sit with my new paint box and make pretty pictures. So I agreed that I wouldn't mind going there. I don't remember war being mentioned or why there was a need for children to leave the towns. I was also used to being pretty independent and finding my way around from one relative's house to another, so this sounded like quite a good adventure. Later a man came to our school and amid great hilarity he fitted us all with gas masks and showed us the correct way to put them on. They smelled strongly of rubber and the eye pieces were prone to steam up. We were also given cardboard boxes to keep them in with a strap to sling them over our shoulders and we had to learn by heart our National Identity number.

A few days later the whole school assembled at Heaton Station, a suburban stop on the line north, and amid much confusion and a lot of crying, we were loaded onto the train. I don't remember much about the actual journey, which wasn't all that long as Morpeth, our destination, was only fifteen miles away. It was a small town that straddled the Great North Road, and was sited on the River Wansbeck. We had often driven through it and my Uncle Harry owned a wooden bungalow on the far side of the golf course where we had enjoyed family gatherings.

I do remember the train arriving at the station, however. Several ladies with lists on clipboards were fending off eager women intent on picking out the children they wished to have in their homes – probably the ones that looked least likely to have nits. After beating them off we were organised into groups in the care of each volunteer and, armed with our gas masks and our little suitcases, we set off down the hill leading from the station. I recognised where we were at the bottom for this was the road we took to get to the bungalow. We passed the police station, which at Morpeth is like a large medieval castle, then swung off to cross the pedestrian bridge over the river. Eventually, when we reached the first houses, there would be a knock on the door and when it was answered the list was consulted and the requisite number of children delivered. This caused some upset from time to time as brothers and sisters refused to be parted and some fairly brisk exchanges took place. After what seemed a very long time, only three of us were left. We crossed the river again towards a row of terraced houses stretching away from the river. At number 1, Auburn Place all three of us were deposited with a somewhat bemused elderly and childless widow. She was very kind but one of our number left the next day to stay with her grandparents who lived in the town and who'd been thwarted in their efforts to retrieve her at the station. Audrey Bruce and I remained. Mrs Wassle's house was very nice and she had gas lighting which flared up with the aid of a mantle, something I had never seen before.

The next morning we were sat down to write our new addresses on the ready-stamped and addressed postcards with which we had been provided. We were taken to the postbox to send them off so that our families would know where we were. This done, we settled in and in the evening Mrs Wassle produced an orange each for Audrey and I which she warmed in front of the fire in the front room, but mine got a bit burnt.

The next day was Sunday, so I suggested to Audrey that I should take her to visit my grandmother at the bungalow where I knew she had gone to stay. We set off back through the town and as we passed the police station, loud sirens sounded. We had no means of knowing what it meant so we pressed on up the road, through the churchyard at the top and, skirting the golf course, we walked along a disused railway track until we reached the edge of the golf course and the fence we had to climb over to reach the back of the bungalow. To my surprise, most of the family were there, and my surprise was nothing to their consternation when I turned up in their midst. I suppose they must have been listening to the announcement on the radio that we were at war with Germany, but I didn't actually hear it myself. Audrey and I were bundled into one of the cars and delivered back to Mrs Wassle. Whether it was this experience of disappearing children, or whether, as I was told, Mrs Wassle

11

left to stay with a relative in Australia, the fact remains that Audrey and I were split up and I was moved further up Auburn Place to number eleven. These houses were a bit meaner than those at the other end of the street. Number eleven was actually an upstairs flat with no bathroom, an outside lavatory and a lot of people. Mrs Archibald was a widow; her younger child, Betty, was two years younger than me, Edwin was my age and Thomas, at 11 years old, was two years older. There was also an unspecified gentleman who occasionally came and went in Mrs Archibald's large front bedroom, but who didn't eat with us and whose name I never found out. The two boys shared the small front bedroom and Betty and I shared a bed in the small back bedroom. I never considered this place a comedown when set against my own home as I was used to similar flats where some of my maternal relatives lived. Auntie May and Uncle Alfie had just such a flat towards the end of Biddlestone Road, but the end three pairs of flats were owned by Grandpa Cleminson, who had a workshop at the end in the back lane where he would do the work to keep them all in good repair. The big difference was that Auntie May's flat had a bathroom although the toilet was in the back yard. At Auburn Place the tin bath came out on a Friday night and we were all bathed in turn in the same water. I quite enjoyed it rather than the nightly bath Florence had given me.

My doll's pram had come with me but I had to defend it against the boys who liked nothing better than to give each other rides in it at high speed up and down the lane at the back of the row of houses. Betty and I would knit clothes for our dolls. Hers was called Cora, and mine, for some unknown reason, was John.

School was at the other end of town and we evacuees were squeezed in with the local children, but soon this ceased to be a problem as bit by bit, the parents of Newcastle took their children home again. Eventually I was transferred to

12

the church school at the other end of town and used to reach it by walking along the river, over the stepping stones and up a little alleyway to the top of town. On my first day our schoolmaster asked for my address. When I told him he barked ferociously at me, 'Auburn?' Not knowing what he meant I was silent until some bright spark stuck her hand up and supplied the answer, 'Ginger, sir.' This, I discovered, was his way of keeping us on our toes.

Eventually, only a rather weak-minded brother and sister and myself were left out of the whole school. The reason for this lay back at home. Florence had been drafted in to war work of some kind (I never found out what) and my father let our house to distant relatives, the Curleys. The husband, Uncle Phil, was occasionally up at Scapa Flow and they had a son, Philip and daughter, Anne. On the death of both my grandparents, Ethel had been left the house, Woodburn, plus Victoria House and a house nearby, probably because she had cared for her parents while Marian had been helped financially to set up her kennels. She still lived at Woodburn, but my dad moved in with them. Ethel went to work at the local post office and later got promotion and was transferred to one at Whitley Bay, so there was no one able – or perhaps willing – to look after me. Sometimes I would plead with my father to let me come home, but to no avail. His lorries had been taken over by the authorities, although for years they stood in a yard off the road near where we lived. Dad, who would have been 37 at the beginning of the war, suffered from duodenal ulcers so instead of being drafted into the forces he was put in charge of the AFS (the Auxiliary Fire Service), as the fire service was known at that time, for the whole of Newcastle. Maryon, of course, went on breeding her dogs.

Morpeth is a small market town set alongside the River Wansbeck, which flows in generous curves through the valley. Approaching it from Newcastle in the south, the road passes the golf course on the left and the country road leading to my uncle's bungalow, and the cottage hospital on the right. As it dips down towards the town, the church with its yew trees and graveyard is on the left where, I remember being told, the young suffragette who threw herself in front of the King's horse, is buried. I have no idea if this is true. Lined by a high wall on the left and pleasantly wide grass verges on the right, it passes the end of the road leading to the station. (I have often noticed that most of the railway stations I have known were on top of a hill.) The road then plunges down towards the river and the large bridge carrying the Great North Road over it; the police station with its battlements is on the right and nearby is the school I first attended. At this point the road executes a swift dog-leg to the left and along it were the principal shops: Woolworth's, that centre of delight, Maynard's the large sweet shop and the Maypole, a grocer's. Also upstairs was Betty's café where occasionally, when my father and some of the aunts descended to see me, we would go for tea and cakes.

At the far end of the road, the main road made another dog-leg turn to the right and continued on up the hill, past the Church of England near the top and so on its way to Alnwick and the North. However, at the bottom of this road at the point where the sharp right turn occurred, a smaller road carried straight on, skirting round a high stone tower, the purpose of which I never found out. Along this road were houses, the Catholic church, the sweet shop where we bought liquorice boot laces and bulls' eyes, and where we played hop scotch and blind man's buff in the evenings. As it grew dark, the lamplighter would come armed with his short ladder and his ever-burning flame to light the lamps along the street.

There was also a hall on the left where the Scouts and Guides assembled and for a short while I wore the uniform of a Brownie and learned to tie granny and reef knots. One

14

of the boys at the Scouts whom I knew slightly told me one night he had something to show me. We walked to the end of the road where a rough path led down to the river on the near side and there he told me the Scout master had told them how babies were made. He persuaded me to lie down and then he lay on top of me, and as, fully clothed, we lay nose to nose he said this was how it was done. Fortunately for me, his instruction had gone no further, and we got up and I avoided him thereafter. It must have been about this time that I wet the bed for the one and only time of my life, to the jeering scorn of Edwin, Mrs Archibald's youngest son.

Since then I have always felt that the modern rise in teenage pregnancies has a lot to do with sex education that is given too early.

At the end of this road on the left was an orchard and then the bridge designed for lighter traffic and pedestrians. On the far side almost straight ahead was Auburn Place, where I lived, a street of terraced houses running up the hill towards the woods with pavement at one side for access to the front doors and a rutted lane at the back where the back yards abutted. At the front was another orchard and I remember that first spring when the apple blossoms bloomed and above we could hear the drone of aeroplanes. I didn't know it at the time, but I dare say they were being flown by pilots in training at the air force base nearer the coast. To the right of the bridge on the far side, the houses stood back behind a wide grassy stretch of ground dotted with large trees where a circus came once and a monkey bit me. At the far end the stepping stones led across the river and a rough path went up to the North Road at the top near the church. I was sent to this church on a Sunday morning and enjoyed the hymns, soon learning them off by heart. I particularly enjoyed the background rumble of the organ which accompanied and emphasised the solemnity of the Creed. The minister would always pray for the Forces and for victory over the enemy and even at that age I know it occurred to me to wonder what God made of it, for no doubt the Germans were uttering exactly the same prayers. Behind the church was the little church school where, on frozen winter afternoons, before we left for the day, we would throw lots of water across the playground to make a satisfactory slide the next day.

Nearby was the library, where I was a frequent visitor and where I was fortunate enough to stumble across a book called *The Secret Garden* and absorb its magic. Reading was my delight then and always has been since. I was once told that when my mother was a young girl she would curl up in a corner with a book and become dead to the world. So it was with me, and, especially at life's difficult times, it was always possible to escape into the world of fiction.

Back at the bridge and on the left-hand side was a pathway built above the river and below the woods which covered the hill, which led down to the more cultivated areas of wide parkland and flower beds. Further down the river was a weir which made it deeper at this point and there were ducks and, in the summer, rowing boats to be hired. However, returning to the main road where it swept up north and out of the town, a smaller road led off to the left. On the corner stood the Town Hall and beside it on this side road was the cinema where, if one had the wherewithal, the Saturday afternoon matinee was a source of pure delight. This road then widened out into a large market square with a foot bridge at the end which crossed the river at the point where the boats were for hire. During the war years, the travellers, or gypsies, who toured the country with fun fairs, were unable to move around the country. I don't know whether this was because of regulations or the unavailability of petrol – I suspect the former – but here their little group of caravans stayed and their roundabouts and hoopla stalls attracted the youth of the town. I became friendly with Rosie, who lived in one of the caravans, and we would roam the woods above the river with several of her disreputable friends. Hours of fun were had with a rope tied to the high branch of a tree which could be swung out over the hillside. The one in flight would then call out the name of a favoured one who would leap on as the rope swung back and the two would hurtle back and forth. At the top of the hill were fields where turnips could be picked and roughly washed off. The taste of sweet raw turnip still takes me back to those days.

I learned to swim, after a manner, in the river under the bridge and so life was full and I did not miss my home, with my doll's house, the birthday parties and family Christmases. The family would visit from time to time and I wrote a letter home every week.

Once we were all up at the bungalow for the weekend, which was a rather cramped affair. There was only one bedroom, lined with bunk beds, where we all slept and in the middle of the night there was an almighty blast which brought us all tumbling out of our beds. Panic ensued as the bedclothes thrown to the floor prevented the door from being opened, but when we got out there was very little to see except that in the kitchen, where a tall kitchen dresser stood, laden with china, the huge tea urn, which normally sat on the highest shelf, had been bodily lifted to crash down on the floor without touching a single piece of china. Later we learned that an enemy plane had mistakenly dropped a mine (probably intended for the sea near Blyth) into a field near us, where it had detonated. Down in the town the windows of the Singer shop on the corner were blown out, along with many others.

One other memory remains. It was often my job to take the battery called the accumulator to a shop to be topped up in order to run the wireless at Mrs Archibald's. I remember listening with disbelief as the proprietor told me that it was possible to have a box at home which would produce films just like the pictures. Well, I don't suppose you would have believed him either.

So childhood in Morpeth was fun – I had freedom and independence, no one asked me where I was going or what I had been doing, and I kept my thoughts to myself.

2

It is many years since I sat my eleven-plus exam. Oddly enough, it was over forty years later that I found I had actually passed. I always thought that my father had had to pay for me to go to high school (even though I don't suppose it was free), and I never thought to ask. I suppose that within our rather fractured family, each one thought someone else had told me, and with the upheaval of war years I expect that, manlike, my father just forgot. In any event, Auntie Ethel took me to Keswick, to where the school was evacuated, to have my interview. I don't remember much of it, but the next event was the buying of my school uniform at Raymond Barnes, the school outfitters. The uniform consisted of a brown gym tunic with a cream-coloured square necked blouse, brown blazer with school badge. Brown knee socks and brown shoes completed the winter outfit. In summer we wore brown-and-cream-checked cotton dresses and panama hats. Winter hats were felt ones with the school band above the brim. To this day I can't abide wearing a hat, and yet, oddly, I still like the colour brown. Added to this was a hockey stick, a tennis racket and a swim suit. Oh yes ... and brown knickers. Suitably equipped, I was packed off to Keswick.

The school was called the Central Newcastle High School, or CNHS for short, and we were made aware that it was part of the Girls' Public Day School Trust, whatever that meant. I never did find out, which just goes to show that grand titles are rarely self-explanatory. At Keswick, we shared premises with the Keswick High School and were known locally and quite naturally as the Brown Bombers. (Joe Louis fans will appreciate the reference.) Next door to the school was the pencil factory with its pervading smell of cedar.

I don't remember first arriving there or what my mode of transport was, but the first house at which I stayed was situated up the hill away from the lakeside and was owned by Mrs Pettitt, an elderly widow, and her middle-aged daughter, Miss Pettitt. Miss Pettitt also owned and ran a large and well-stocked gift shop in the town. I really can't imagine why they thought it would be a good idea to take in an evacuee, as you couldn't have found two women less well-equipped to care for an eleven-year-old girl. While I was there they also bought a spaniel puppy, an appealing little dog. The poor thing disgraced itself on the hall carpet and had its nose rubbed in the resultant mess, which no doubt turned it into a nervous wreck. Once, feeling hungry, I helped myself to a couple of biscuits in the pantry and was duly scolded when I was found out. It made me wonder what they might want to rub *my* nose in.

I hadn't immediately made any friends at school, so at weekends I would roam the woods as I had been used to doing in Morpeth. Thus I came across one of the most delightful experiences of my childhood. Beyond the row of houses where I lived there was a lane and then rough meadows which led up to a wood set against a sloping hill. I spent a lot of time in this wood with its autumn smells; at school we were making miniature gardens with a piece of mirror in the centre to simulate a pond, and mosses and toadstools around about. In my search for the most colourful toadstools, I roamed higher and higher up the hill, until one day I came to a jumble of rocks at the top. Working my way around them, I clambered on to a sheltered ledge where, spread out before me, was the whole of Derwentwater, with its islands, its beaches and woods sweeping down to the water's edge. It was south facing, and often I climbed up there to enjoy the peaceful scene. I sometimes wonder how many other people have discovered that spot in the intervening years. I expect the meadow is full of housing now, and if it has been found, perhaps it is featured on the tourist trail complete with tea room, gift shop and eager Japanese tourists with the latest technology in camcorders. And if so, why not, for why should I deny anyone else the everlasting pleasure of that memory (and here, of course, Wordsworth springs to mind) which is the bliss of solitude.

I didn't stay long at the Pettitts. I doubt if there was much sorrow at our parting on either side, as we were not suited to one another. I do remember my arrival at the railway station at the beginning of the next term – we had been home for Christmas – and once more I found myself staggering down the road from the station, this time with a large suitcase. A very kind gentleman offered to carry it for me and so I arrived at Mrs Thwaite's. She lived in a council house on an estate which lay on a rise between the town and the lake. It was a small semi-detached house but it held an alarming number of people. Apart from myself, there were also Stella and Jean, who were in my form at school, and Joan, who was a couple of years older than us. We had the sole use of the front room for our meals and doing our homework, except occasionally during the better weather when the odd visitor was taken in for bed and breakfast. Fortunately for us, visitors were few and far between during the war years, but I remember one famous occasion when six girls shared a double bed lying head to tail like sardines There was a Mr Thwaites, a slip of a man, and the two daughters of the house. Outside in the garden was a variety of sheds, which probably catered for the rest of the inhabitants, but this was out of bounds to us. There was a sister and her rather feeble-minded son Freddie, who drooled and didn't say very much; there was Frankie, her nephew who had been evacuated to her from Birkenhead; and, of course, her two daughters, Elsie and Audrey. If I had felt lonely before, this was now an overabundance of company, but I have to say that as an only child I revelled in it.

When I was six or seven years old I used to pray at night that God would give me a baby brother or sister and I would lie right on the edge of my little blue bed to show God that there would be plenty of room for another one. I didn't realise that with my mother gone, this was not going to happen and it was a great disappointment to me and strained my faith in God. Now it was like all my Christmases come at once and I revelled in this swarming mass of people crammed into the little house. Over sixty years on I have lost touch with all the others apart from Stella, with whom I keep up an intermittent correspondence. As she says, at our age it is largely a question of an exchange of symptoms.

Stella was and is very clever, with beautifully formed hand-writing. She was the only daughter and the middle child of her parents, with an elder brother Donald and a younger called Stanley. Jean was the eldest daughter of a Methodist minister and had two younger sisters. Joan, being older, did not figure so highly in our lives and I knew nothing of her family.

Our school was not the only one to be based in Keswick, Rhodean School for Girls had taken over a very large and plush hotel on the edge of town, and they were occasionally to be seen walking in strictly regulated crocodiles around the town.

School was enjoyable. Our French teacher was called Miss Sorrel and we were initiated into that language with the memorable phrases of 'la plume de ma tante' and 'ouvre la porte' or alternatively 'la fenêtre'. I never really got to grips with the masculine and feminine gender of words, much less the grammar with its past imperfect, but on my first visit to France some forty years later I found I had retained enough phrases and vocabulary to be of use. Miss Sorrel, who later unaccountably exchanged her name for Mrs Sidebottom, must have done a good job.

22

Our geography teacher was called Miss Horne, and her grandfather had been the master of a sailing ship, and used to regale her with stories of sailing around the Horn of South America. She also introduced us to the world of the *National Geographic* magazine, which brought the things she taught us blazingly to life. Geography was one of my favourite subjects and gave me a lifelong interest in the rest of the world and the placing of various countries within it. Miss Horne also filled in as needlework teacher and in those days of rationing, whatever we made had to be of some use. Consequently we were set to making a pair of summer knickers in brown-and-white checked cotton. There were two sewing machines, hand operated, but one could not gravitate to them until one's hand sewing had passed muster. Alas, I never reached those pinnacles; my hand sewing was terrible and on one never-to-be-forgotten occasion, Miss Horne looked at my work in disgust and tore the whole seam from end to end. Having sweated blood and tears over that work, I had no wish to have it repeated, so when it came to stitching the hems, I enlisted the help of Audrey, who was able to place endless neat little stitches exactly where she wanted them to go. When I produced this wonderful piece of work, Miss Horne must have been well aware that it did not spring from my own efforts, but perhaps she took pity on me, because after a very long look, she made no comment.

Our English teacher was Miss Forrest and English lessons were a joy. I had learned to read and write at a very early age – before I started school, actually – and our early classes had always included spelling and vocabulary on a regular basis. Thus I was well grounded, and always an avid reader, I enjoyed the literature we studied. I think at that time we did not go on to the science subjects in the upper third class. It may have been that the facilities being shared with Keswick High School were not sufficient for us all. I don't really know, but I expect that allowances had to be made.

23

Our teachers were all referred to as 'mistresses' of course, and our headmistress was Miss Leale, a quiet lady with an underlying strength of character who never raised her voice.

That winter we had very heavy snow falls and we went sledging on the small golf course between the town and the lake. There was also a small kiosk just inside the park gates where there was a roulette wheel on the wall. It would take pennies and the balls were released and then sent off with the aid of a pull-back spring. If you were lucky, they might drop into the right hole and you would get your penny back, but after losing a large proportion of my pocket money, I decided that although it was quite a thrilling pastime, I had no wish to lose my money, and so I never became an inveterate gambler. Another slot machine was on the high street, and for a few coppers you could get a small packet of Woodbine cigarettes and some matches. We would take these into the outside toilets and puff away in an amateurish fashion, feeling very grown-up and daring.

School lunches had to be taken at another venue further up the High Street where we had to wait in a room without any windows until the meal was ready. We would douse the lights and play 'murders' where, after a terrible shriek, the lights would be put back on and we had to guess who had 'done for' the body on the floor. The meals were generally of a poor standard, the so-called meat being mainly bones and gravy with very little in it of substance, but had we ever complained, which we didn't, I dare say we would have been told briskly that there was a war on. (Not that that had escaped our notice, or else why were we in Keswick?)

The River Greta swept around the back of the town and my friends and I spent a lot of time watching the salmon attempting to jump up and over the weir. The grey stone houses and the greenish-coloured local slates blended well with the surrounding mountains and always gave a clear-cut and ordered feel to the town.

In the summer we were taken down to the lake to swim away from where the tourist rowing boats were drawn up on the way to Friars Crag. Further along towards the Bassenthwaite end of the lake was a jetty into the deeper water and here we could splash and swim. I remember going there on one occasion when a thunderstorm was in the offing. The water in the lake was warm, and rose and fell in oily swells, the air became oppressive and still and eventually the rain came down in torrents and there was such a feeling of exhilaration in being so much a creature of the water, both in it and under it.

We could choose which church we wished to attend, and although I used to accompany my grandfather to the Baptist church on Heaton Road as a small child, I revelled in the choice and took to trying them all. My favourite, for its beauty rather than its services was Crossthwaite church, the C of E church at the head of the lake. The large Presbyterian church was imposing if rather cold and the Methodist church felt welcoming.

One half term when we had a few days off, I decided to go and visit my aunt by marriage on the farm above the lake at Bassenthwaite. Aunt Ada and Aunt Belle were the sisters of the young man who had gone to Australia and sent for my Aunt Gladys as his bride. My cousin Marian was staying with them at the time and attending the village school so, unannounced, I caught the bus from Keswick and got off at the end of the long lane that led uphill to the farm. It was a delight to walk up as it went through a small scented tree-lined valley at one point, where wild strawberries could be had for the taking. So tiny, and yet such a luscious taste. The farm at the top was windswept with a wide selection of barns and outhouses adjoining and surrounding it. The dairy was always spotless and cool and the stone shelves would hold wide earthenware dishes of milk from which the thick cream was skimmed. Next to them was the butter churn which I loved to take a hand at turning and see the miracle of the butter eventually thumping around the barrel when it was taken out and shaped and patted with the butter paddles. The remaining buttermilk would be fed to the calves and I loved the task of weaning the young animals by bringing the bucket of butter milk to them, putting my hand into their mouths and feeling them suck with babyish enthusiasm, then guiding their heads down into the liquid so that they drew the milk up for themselves. It never ceased to amaze me how quickly they got the hang of it, and even now I remember the feel of their warm mouths and their rough tongues. Upstairs in the house, in one of the unused bedrooms, the floors would be spread with newspapers and the season's apple harvest would be laid out to dry off before being wrapped and stored for winter. The huge kitchen was warm and comfortable and I envied Marian living in this house. On this occasion, Auntie Ada was surprised to see me and explained that she had to go to Cockermouth market to sell her butter and eggs while Marian had to go to school. I could choose to go with her or with Marian, so I chose to go to the school. It was quite a long walk and the teacher must have been surprised to have another pupil, but she made room for me and I had a very enjoyable day. The highlight for me was the singing class, when we sang the 'Skye Boat Song'. I must have had quite a strong voice even then, as I remember the teacher walking up and down past me as I sang, probably wondering where all the noise was coming from.

Then it transpired that my father had put my name down for Barrow House, and at the start of the next school year, there was a place for me. Barrow House was a private hotel which the school was leasing. It lay on the north shore of the lake just before Lodore House and falls. It also had a waterfall at the back of the house where the electricity generator lived, and which occasioned ominous flickering of the lights when the water ran low. About fifty girls could be housed here and we had dormitories with bunk beds, a large dining room and a library and study for doing homework. My friend Jean was also there and we used to beg some flour and buy a tin of golden syrup and some matches. Thus equipped, we would climb up the hill at the back of the house above the waterfall and up onto the moors. Here there was a bridge and a ruined barn beside it; we would get water from the stream, light a fire and mix our 'dampers' in a purloined pan from the kitchen. Any stick would do to wrap the dough around and we would sit over our smoking fire and eventually, when patience ran out, eat our half-cooked dampers smeared with golden syrup. The beauty of it was that all the stickiness could be washed off, and the washing-up done in the cold racing stream. And then we could relax and gaze across the beautiful view of the bridge and the lake. It was only in later years that I discovered we were enjoying a famous beauty spot, the Ashness Bridge.

Hallowe'en saw us draping blankets down the sides of our bunks and having midnight feasts with candles in hollowed-out turnips. Fortunately nothing caught fire. In the hard winter, the lake froze over and we skated and slid on its surface. To begin with, we used to walk back to Barrow House from Keswick in a 'crocodile', but later on we had a bus and we used to sing 'The woman stood at the churchyard door...' with great gusto as we drove back along the lakeside.

They were very happy times, one that any schoolgirl who has read Angela Brazil would have recognised, and I would happily have stayed there to the end of my school days, but it was not to be. The bombing of the north of England had declined somewhat, and the school in Newcastle, which had originally been requisitioned for some war purpose, was now available, and so we were to be brought back. It seemed it wasn't all over completely however, because as our train returned to Newcastle in the dark, we had to stop some way outside the city for some time as there was an air raid in progress. The windows were all blacked out and we were forbidden to fiddle with the blinds, but we could hear the explosions and we knew that if the furnace in the engine could be seen by the enemy, we could become a target. But one thing I learned at that time was that young people have very little fear. We shuddered among ourselves and worked ourselves up into a mild hysteria, but really we had no concept of what the consequences of an attack might be.

And so we settled into our school, a new experience for most of us, and also had to make a space for ourselves back in our old homes. For me this was not easy. I had left the home which I shared with my father and Florence three years before, but I returned to my grandparents' house next door, the house now owned by my Auntie Ethel and which was shared with her sister, Auntie Maryon and my father. And I was homesick for Keswick.

My one consolation was Ross my dog, who, having belonged to my aunt, now became my own and faithful companion.

3

The decision to return to Newcastle turned out to be somewhat premature. The air raids, if anything, had increased, and where beforehand I had had very little experience of the war, that was to change. Air-raid shelters were the norm and there were a number of types. The most famous was the Anderson Shelter, one of which we had in the garden at Woodburn. This was constructed by digging a rectangular hole about four feet deep, and then erecting a curved roof made out of corrugated iron. The ends were filled in, one end being blocked off and the other end having a door with steps down into the interior. The walls were lined with wood and the earth that had been dug out to form the hole was piled over the corrugated iron and overlaid with the grass sods. Inside were bunk beds and we used to keep a tin containing candles and matches and, as the interiors were reasonably dry, an assortment of bedding. In the house we would have a small suitcase packed with emergency clothing and important documents which could be snatched up when necessary. As you can imagine, the prospect in winter of staggering down the garden was not appealing, so the back-up plan was to shelter in the cupboard under the stairs, which was reckoned to be the safest spot.

At Auntie Elsie's flat, she had a large table of strengthened steel in Peter's bedroom at the back of the flat under which he had his bed and where they could all gather when the sirens sounded. Outside in their street there was also a large brick reinforced building where at least twenty people could take shelter. However, these were vulnerable if there was a

29

direct hit, which did happen in one street, with a great loss of life. Of course, if the raid took place during the day, then shelters were available around the town. One of our great discoveries was the shelter in the grounds of the Hancock Museum sited on the slope above the Haymarket. One day we went into the shelter there and discovered that there was a tunnel that disappeared into the distance. When we followed it we found that it exited outside the church right in the Haymarket. It seemed that these tunnels had been opened up as shelters but that originally they had been used to run coal down to the quayside, or so we were told. These were all boarded up again after the war, but I dare say they are still there under the ground; no doubt some of them would be found when they built the new Metro through to the Haymarket many years later.

The air-raid sirens wailing were usually the first indication we had that there would be a raid in the offing, but sometimes a lone plane would sneak in undetected. I was with Auntie Ethel visiting a friend of hers who lived at Cullercoats, on the coast. I was sent off to amuse her young son and we went up to the bathroom to sail his little boats, and as I idly gazed out of the bathroom window I saw a plane come down low and a stick of bombs fall out from under it before it veered off and flew away. I raced downstairs to tell what I had seen but by then, of course, the explosions had been felt and we packed up and came home on the train. As we came to the cutting where one of the stations was situated, we saw the damage above us where a bomb had hit a house.

Our house, Woodburn, was situated in a valley a mile or so from the centre of the city. On one side the wooded slopes stretched for a mile or two and was a famous beauty spot called Jesmond Dene. Our house was situated at the side of the main road to the coast which swept down the hill and around and up the other side, and where the tram cars clanked and growled their way up and down. Stretched across the

30

valley was Armstrong Bridge, named after Lord Armstrong, the munitions millionaire. The bridge was high across the valley and supported on slender iron pillars, so was not suitable for heavy traffic and only cars were allowed to go across it. At the other side of the road lay Armstrong Park, which adjoined Woodburn and the two houses next door built by my father and my uncle. This was also well wooded and here and there were springs and wells fed by underground streams. One night the bombers came and trying, no doubt, to destroy the bridge and/or the road which was the main artery to the coast, they dropped a string of bombs across the valley. We were under the stairs on that occasion and felt the force of the explosions. Fortunately, they missed both the road and the bridge but hit a small cottage on the far side of the valley while the remaining bombs formed craters all the way across. The shift in the rock layers meant that all the wells dried up as the underground streams found new ways to the surface and water trickled willy-nilly all around the park. On another occasion we had a stick of incendiaries rain down on our back garden which did not ignite and did no harm.

The worst raid, however, was one which scored a hit on the goods station in town. Its damaged walls stood for many years afterwards until the town planners decided what to do with that area, but I remember the roads roundabout being slippery and green with the mould from the fats and sugars that had been part of the loads which were blasted to pieces.

Mostly, the war was about feeling cold in winter, only having nine inches of water in the bath, feeling hungry and having to eat uninteresting meals made from whatever could be got from the shops and the everlasting queues outside. Collecting the rations from the butcher's shop and from the grocer's needed the patience of a saint and the resulting minuscule portions hardly seemed worth the effort, except that that was all we had.

Bananas, of course, were unheard of, but it was possible to buy a small bottle of banana essence which, when added to mashed sweetened potato, tasted like something resembling the real thing. Oranges and lemons were also impossible to obtain and autumn was looked forward to for our home-grown fruits of plums, apples and pears. When the plum season was on most of us had diarrhoea from gorging ourselves in the absence of anything sweeter. I had a bit of a sweet tooth, but strangely, I detested sugar in my tea. I think this was because when I lived at Mrs Archibald's in Morpeth, she used to put sugar in all our teas when she poured them out. I then neglected to stir mine and took a dislike to the syrupy brew at the bottom of the cup. Our sweet ration was $^{3}/_{4}$lb. per month and greatly looked forward to. Potatoes ranked high on our diet and one of my favourites was potato soup with plenty of chopped parsley in it for flavour. Our meals were bland and uninteresting as, of course, we had no access to spices.

By a sheer fluke, no close member of our family was in the forces. Uncle Harry was born in 1897 so was too old and ran the local Home Guard. My father, was in his late thirties and was put in charge of the Fire Service in Newcastle as Column Officer. Uncle Stan, of course, had died and my aunts were unmarried. The husband of my mother's sister, Elsie, worked on the shipyards and I never knew why May's husband, Uncle Alfie, was not in the Forces. I think he worked in the Civil Service, but at nights he played the violin at a dance band at the Oxford, a well-known dance hall in Newcastle. My Grandmother Trobe had two surviving sisters; Auntie Annie was married to Uncle Tom and had two daughters. They had lived in India at one time but it seems they returned to England under a cloud, although I never found out what had happened. Their surname was Nicholson and Uncle Tom sailed on merchant ships that plied the dangerous passage to Archangel in Russia. He was a fat jolly fellow of whom I was very fond and he used to joke that they only took him along as ballast. Auntie Cissie was married to Uncle Charlie and they had two daughters, Marian and Sheila Curley. By a generational fluke, Sheila was only a year older than me and her father worked on the fish quay at North Shields, and Dogger Bank featured large in their conversations. The Curleys had two close friends, Jack and Bobby Sharp, who visited regularly and made a great fuss of Sheila. I used to be very envious as they bought her very expensive toys such as perfectly designed toy sports cars which ran on clockwork. She also had a huge doll's house that they delighted in furnishing for her from the best toy shop in Newcastle.

The only other person I knew who was involved directly in the war was Louis Inganni. His mother, a widow, had lived near my grandparents on Heaton Park Road where she was the local midwife who delivered me when I was born at home. Louis and his brother were regular visitors at my grandparents' home and were well thought of by my maiden aunts. Louis was shot down from his plane in a sortie over Germany and spent several years of the war as a prisoner-of-war.

War was a way of life. We would discuss in gruesome detail what we would do to Hitler if we caught him and I was convinced that if the Germans invaded they wouldn't be able to catch me as I would hide out in the Park and the Dene. News was sparse, and in the evenings my father and Auntie Ethel would sit in front of the fire with the radio burbling quietly away while Ethel knitted and my father rustled his paper. Bored, I took to taking Ross out to walk and so joined up with my second set of disreputable friends, a gang of lads, with me the only girl, where we would climb trees and race around the park in the dark, each one having a yodelling call by which we could identify each other. Derek Powton's father owned a butcher's shop on Chillingham Road and was an amateur wrestler; one of the lads was Chinese – his family owned a laundry at the far end of Chillingham Road – and Thomas Barnes and Edmund Ions's fathers were in the Forces. We would tie ropes to the tree branches and risk life and limb by swinging out over the stream, and we climbed up inside the hollow metal struts of Armstrong Bridge and walked daredevil along its parapet. In the autumn we set the dried grass alight on the slopes on the far side of the valley and in the winter we sledged down them. The best sledging run, however, was on the narrow steep road that bisected Jesmond Dene. Sledging down there once on my cousin Marian's sledge, which had a fancy arrangement of ropes to steer it, I inadvertently pulled the wrong rope and knocked three posts out of the fence edging the road with my head. In the dark, no one noticed and I got up and sledged on, but as I walked back up the hill in the company of some of the others, all of a sudden I couldn't remember where I was and had to sit down for a while. But soon I felt better and, undeterred, carried on sledging, finally returning home with blood all down my collar. I still have a scar there where hair won't grow, and a little later my hair fell out on that side of my head, but eventually grew back again.

School was a different matter. I did not do too well and blundered along, only just coping. I was capable of better, but never could rustle up much enthusiasm. I think perhaps a lot had to do with the fact that no one at home was very interested. My father had his own concerns and Auntie Ethel had never wanted to look after me, so I was left to my own devices. Woodburn, was not a large house; it had originally had two rooms upstairs and two down, but my grandfather had one of the bedrooms divided up into two small rooms with a connecting passage, while at the back of the house he had a single storey built along the length. This provided a kitchen, bathroom and toilet as well as a room used as an office. At the end, reached from outside, was a laundry and the coal-house, leading into the garage. My father had one of the small bedrooms and Auntie Maryon the other. I shared the large bedroom and the double bed with Auntie Ethel.

Marian and Ethel would fight, sometimes physically, and there was always either an atmosphere or a fight going on in the house. My father kept his head down, and as I have said, I used to escape with my friends, probably when I should have been doing my homework. My one friend was Ross, my dog. He would wait for me to come home from school and as I jumped off the tram on the far side of the valley, he would run to meet me with his tail going round in circles and we would joyfully leap around each other. He always came with me when I was sent off to do the shopping and would insist on carrying one of the bags home again. When I was out climbing trees he would spend the time digging holes around the roots and when we annoyed the park keeper by running over the bowling greens, he would happily bark defiance at him while we ran away. Where I went, Ross went. Marian and I would go for a walk through Jesmond Dene on a Sunday, but she also had a dog, a black Chow called Woofles, and Ross and Woofles hated each other. So we had to take it in turns to take our dogs until one Sunday when it was my turn to take Ross, Marian turned up with Woofles. They leapt at each other, both going for the throat and we were powerless to separate them. Fortunately, a couple of men who were passing came and helped us to drag them apart, but they would otherwise have fought to the death.

Auntie Maryon rented the area under the bridge that was part of the ground attached to a house called St Mary's Mount at the top of the valley on the Jesmond side. Here she had the kennels for her dogs and also for a while, she kept a goat and we all grew quite fond of goats' milk. When an air raid was on the dogs seemed to know and as soon as their keen hearing picked up the sounds of the planes, they would set up a banshee, wailing and howling. We also became quite adept at telling what sort of planes were overhead by the sound of their engines. Eventually, Maryon had the chance to buy the house and the land and she moved out of Woodburn and into her own home. It was a very large house with a ballroom on one side, and a sitting room, morning room and butler's pantry on the other. It had huge cellars and a range of kitchens and sculleries at the back. My cousin Marian's stepsister, Joyce, had met an American on the air base where she worked in the WAAF and she was married in the church up the hill and Marian and I were bridesmaids. The reception was held in St Mary's Mount and eventually Joyce went to live on a farm in Idaho from where she would send food parcels long after the war was over but when things were still scarce.

As well as working in the post office, Auntie Ethel was a member of the WVS and remained a member for the rest of her life. Just after the war and during the occupation, she was sent over to work in the NAAFI at Nuremberg for a few months.

My main tasks at home were to do any shopping that was required. Ross and I would toil up the hill and come back loaded with a stone of potatoes and any vegetables on offer, as well as our minuscule rations. Ross, of course, needed feeding, and this was in the days before the invention of convenient, if expensive, tins of dog food. So every fortnight it was my task to collect the bag that was smelly and stiff with blood stains and catch the tram that went over the River Tyne to Gateshead. Half way up the hill on the far side of the river, I would get off the tram and walk down a long dreary road where, in winter months, the cutting wind blew straight from the north from across the river. Down at the foot of the hill was a huge shed where the skin and hide merchants prepared the hides for the leather works. Dressed in old clothes and leather aprons, the men had hands like hams and they used their sharp knives to scrape off loose flesh and cut out the backs of the ears from the skins before layering them with salt. There I would stand until one of them would deign to notice me and I'd ask to have my bag filled with the off cuts for two shillings. Then I lugged the dripping bag back up the hill and onto the tram home. This 'meat' was boiled up for Ross and mixed with loose biscuits which Auntie Marian got wholesale for her dogs. I never minded doing this awful job because I loved my dog so much.

My other big task was to collect the rents. Auntie Ethel owned Victoria House and another house nearby, my father owned the pair of flats where I had been born in Warwick Street and Uncle Harry had a couple of houses nearby. I would do my rounds, collect the rents and mark the rent books and sometimes be asked to call on Mr Williams the plumber, to pay his bill or ask him to undertake some work. I became adept at listening sympathetically to tales of damp kitchens and leaking roofs and promising to tell whoever owned the property.

One night, after Auntie Marian had moved out, we heard a crash and when we got up we found my father had fallen on the stairs and he was vomiting blood. My aunt told me to go downstairs and phone the doctor, which I did with fear and trembling. It seemed he had a stomach ulcer and for several weeks he was confined to bed. Eventually the Fire Service sent him to a convalescent home in Cheshire where later on I went to stay with him. I travelled on my own and caught the train from Newcastle and eventually my father met me in Crewe, from where we went on to the lovely country house where he was staying. I didn't like it very much, however, because it was so flat and I still longed for the mountains and the lakes.

One day I got lost in the house and opened a door by mistake. A young man with a hunted look leapt into his bed and pulled up the clothes, chattering gibberish as he did so.

I think he must have been a victim of shell-shock or some such neurosis, but I don't think he got a bigger fright than I did.

Ross seemed to find it harder and harder to carry the basket home as was his wont, and often I struggled with him, and if he insisted, I would share the load with him. I came home from school one day to an empty and silent house. When Auntie Ethel came home she told me Ross had been put to sleep as he had a growth in his stomach.

A little later I developed jaundice, as we called it – some sort of hepatitis I expect – and I was quite ill and confined to a chair bed in the sitting room. My gang of lads had gone by then, as at fourteen they had left school and were apprentices at places like Parsons and Armstrong's factory. I went back to school again but I lost interest in combing my hair until after some weeks Auntie Ethel noticed and had a hard job combing it out. My school work was bad and I was kept back for a year so that I was no longer in the same form as my friends.

The school must have realised that something was wrong and they arranged for me to be seen by a child psychologist. As usual I was never told the result, but looking back on it I think I was probably suffering from depression. Anyhow, things improved at home somewhat. My dad started to talk to me and he and I would go to the cinema together. I remember going to see *The Four Feathers* and, also memorably, *Gone with the Wind*. On that occasion I even managed to persuade him to stay in the queue to get in. Mostly we went to the cinema at the top of the hill, the Lyric, where we would see whatever the offering was for that week. Sometimes in the middle it would be flashed on the screen that an air raid was in progress and we would have to leave as he would have to return to his duty.

Auntie Ethel had a friend called Jenny Skipsy, another single lady who worked behind the counter at Hollingsworths

Hairdressers in Newcastle, the high-class place of its day. Wednesday was her half-day and she would come to us and Auntie Ethel would bake scones and in the evening we would go to the cinema. Jenny lived with her mother in a tenement block of flats near the barracks and had a tearaway nephew. Once she was ill after drinking a cup of tea and it transpired that the little lad had put wooden clothes pegs in the teapot. The walls of their living room were covered in pictures made with silver paper – I loved to look at them. Poor Jenny, she who never smoked in her life died of throat cancer many years later.

We still managed to have holidays; Auntie Maryon had bought a wooden bungalow on the road to Allenheads, and weeks before we were due to go, Auntie Ethel would pack a huge trunk with bedding and other necessities and the carrier would come and take it to the bungalow. On the day we went, carrying a suitcase each, we would catch the tram to Central Station and walk up the road to the bus station, where we would catch the bus to Hexham. There we would pause for a cup of tea while we waited for the Allenheads bus which would take us higher and higher into the hills. Through Allendale and half way to Allenheads we would get off at Sparty Lea. Lugging our cases, we would stagger down the rutted farm road and once in the house, we would struggle with the paraffin stove and light the fire. Sometimes my cousins would come too, as well as other members of the family, and we children would roam the hills, build dams in the streams and help with the hay making.

Auntie Maryon also had a cottage at Nenthead, a couple of valleys further over. It had belonged to my grandfather's sister, Auntie Allie, who had bought it after the First World War. She and Uncle Jim would motor up there but after he died she sold it to Maryon. The cottage was built in the 1600s we later found, and the ground floor had originally been meant for the owner's sheep or cows. Part of it was now a garage and in the pitch-black lower room was built a little wooden edifice that held, joy of joys, a flush toilet, complete with spiders. Entrance to the upstairs living rooms was by an outside stone staircase with a wide terrace at the front door. This led straight into the living room with a large range where the kettle could be boiled. Beyond this room to the right and up a step was the only bedroom, while to the left was the room called the kitchen as it had a sink and cold water tap and a rickety table holding an electric hot-plate. In the nether regions of the room was a single bed. Pretty basic you would think, but it was amazing how many of us would be squeezed in and how much fun we had striding the moors and playing in the streams.

And then, suddenly, the news became interesting. For years we had been used to signs painted on fences saying 'Second Front Now' but at last it happened. France was invaded and we had our maps stuck up on the walls with flags showing where the Allies were. Americans flooded our streets with their nylons and their chewing gum and then as we waited with baited breath, we were told it was all over. Bonfires had been prepared in advance and Marian and I roamed the streets all night joining one or another celebration, until at midnight we linked arms with the crowd and danced down Pilgrim Street doing the Pallais Glide. The favourite song was 'When the Lights Go On Again' because at last we could take down the blackout and have headlights showing on the cars again without the shout of 'Put that light out, don't you know there's a war on?'

4

So the war in Europe was at an end, but we had little idea of what the future might hold. *Before the war* – that Shangri La of children's birthday parties with jellies and cakes, of Christmas mornings with presents and large family gatherings, of being taken to Amos Atkinson's on Northumberland Street to buy my shoes and have my feet examined on their X-ray machine to ensure the fit was right – all this was gone. Boxing Day, when the family en masse took seats in the circle at the Theatre Royal for the pantomime, when I wore my best dress and Auntie Ethel took her opera glasses in a small velvet bag ... now the Good Fairy had come along and waved her magic wand but instead of the pumpkin being turned into a coach, the coach had disappeared and was replaced by this dreary landscape of food shortages and 'utility' clothing and furniture.

Of course, it was not all over, there was still the war in the Far East to be finalised. Then came the atomic bomb and pictures of Hiroshima and Nagasaki and our lives would never be the same again. The celebrations for the end of that war in Japan were muted as we faced the realities of that dreadful power. News, of course, was limited to the newspapers and the newsreels in those days before television, but the images of shattered cities in Europe and lines of dispossessed refugees who had lost their homes and their families were stark. Worse was to come as news filtered through of the terrible death camps with pictures of skeletal men and women in striped pyjama-like clothing as they sat and hunted through their clothes for fleas. Later, someone I

41

knew showed me photos he had taken at Belsen when their company had liberated the camp, the shocking heaps of bodies and the gas chambers still piled up with the dead that had not been incinerated.

In Japan, we saw the devastation of complete cities by one bomb, saw the mushroom-shaped cloud and heard of people's eyeballs being melted as they looked up at the plane overhead or had the skin peel off their arms like gloves as people went to help them. We were not at that time to know the terrible underlying damage to succeeding generations as abnormal children were born or the seeds of destruction sown in the survivors. Certainly for our generation there was a horror of war.

Gradually things began to pick up, although it was to be several years before rationing of one sort or another came to an end. Dad bought me a bike, a second-hand one, of course, as new were not to be had for love nor money. I would cycle to school and in the summer Marian and I would cycle to the coast. For years the beaches had been denied to us by rolls of barbed wire and, so we were told, mines, in case of invasion. But now we could go there freely and often did.

Another favourite haunt was the swimming baths in Jesmond where, at the nearby chemist's shop we would buy liquorice root in order to suck out the sweetness even if it gave us diarrhoea. We probably had the healthiest bowels in town.

Reading was still my passion, and at Miss Loffler's drapery shop at the top of the road where I lurked until the shop emptied and I could buy my sanitary towels in privacy, I patronised her little lending library and discovered the joy of Zane Grey and cowboy stories. I would have loved to be a cowboy.

One day Auntie Ethel suggested I should go and join the Junior Air Corps, an organisation for girls which held its meetings in the evening at a local school. In those days one did not disobey adult requests and so in fear and trembling

I presented myself one night and found to my surprise that it was most enjoyable. Our uniform was a grey skirt and jacket and a jaunty little forage cap and we had classes in map reading and navigation. We never got anywhere near an aeroplane, nor even an airfield, but we would be on parade from time to time for special church services, and what I learned turned out to be very useful in later years in finding my way around in strange countries.

Auntie Maryon had for many years rented the area under Armstrong Bridge which belonged to the large house, St Mary's Mount, at the top of the hill and at the end of Jesmond Road. There were a number of disused stables and a large fenced-in run where her dogs exercised, all of which were reached by a steep curving driveway from the main road, so that when the dogs used to howl when an air raid was imminent, the sound would echo up under the bridge. Later my father used this space for his trucks when, after the war, he set up his haulage contractor business once more. Below the kennels and reaching down towards the burn at the foot of the slope were well-tended market gardens cared for by a taciturn old man, while on the slopes up towards the main road and the high retaining wall were huge beds of rhubarb. Towards the end of the war, Auntie Maryon was offered the house and grounds and managed to raise the money to buy it. There was also a gatehouse on the corner of Jesmond Road and a sweeping drive up to the front of the house. It was here of course that Joyce had her reception after her marriage to her American, but the main result for me was that Auntie Maryon moved out of Woodburn and I had my own bedroom at last, as well as a bit of peace and quiet.

My best friend at school, Stella Ritchie, and I would go to the Playhouse, a theatre set on the hillside just opposite the entrance to the kennels, where on a Monday night, entrance price to the current play was reduced as it was treated as a dress rehearsal. We saw some excellent plays there: *Seagulls over Sorrento*, several other Terence Rattigan plays, and on one memorable occasion, Dame Flora Robson in a chilling melodrama in which she played a witness to a murder having been struck dumb with shock and spent most of the play emitting chilling glares until the final *denouement*. Quite spellbinding! She had been educated at our school, I believe, which made her presence even more absorbing.

It wasn't long before we discovered 'the gods' at the Theatre Royal in Newcastle and would cheerfully queue as the buskers entertained us with music or cutting out paper dolls. There we were able to see the ballet; *Coppelia* was a favourite and the operas, *Cav and Pag* as well as *Carmen* and *Madam Butterfly*. It was a rare treat when the D'Oyly Carte arrived in town and we would go to as many as we were able.

Dad asked me to go for walk with him one night. What he had to say should not have come as a surprise to me, because for quite some time he would disappear at weekends without any explanation. As I have said, our family was not given to lengthy explanations, or indeed, any explanations at all, and being a self-obsessed teenager (in the days before the term 'teenager' was coined), it had not occurred to me that anything untoward was going on. I was soon to be informed otherwise. Dad started off by saying that he would always love my mother, which started the alarm bells ringing, but that he had met someone else. They had met while he was serving in the AFS where she had worked as his secretary. There was no question of marriage as she was a deserted wife. She had made the mistake of marrying in haste during the war but the marriage was over and they had separated. It seemed there was no possibility of divorce as May was the one in the wrong by having an affair with my father, and who knows if I would ever have been told of her existence, except that she had given birth to a little girl. She

44

lived with her parents in Alnwick, a town about thirty miles to the north of us where she and her parents kept a pub. I was to go there the next weekend with my father to meet her, but it was to be a secret and I was not to tell anyone else.

It is hard to say after so many years what my reaction was; some shock I expect, confusion certainly; how would this new list of characters fit into our lives, how would I fit into theirs? Was this at last the sister I had always wanted? I was definitely aware that my father, in telling me, wanted my support, and because I loved him, I gave it unconditionally. Had I wished to talk it over with anyone else, I was barred from doing so by his wish for confidentiality, and I kept that confidence until the day he died, when I had no choice but to tell the family what I knew.

The next Sunday we left early in the car my father had bought from Auntie Allie, a 1930 Austin 6, and drove to Alnwick. There I met May and my new sister for the first time. May must have been in her thirties, quite tall and somewhat angular, with a smoker's gravelly voice. It was obvious that she was nervous and wanted to make a good impression on me so I did my best to be friendly. She told me she had called the baby Doreen, because that was her sister-in-law's name and she 'had been very good to her when she had had the baby'. I found this a bit odd and somewhat stickily sentimental and I could never imagine choosing the name of a child of mine on that basis, but needless to say I said nothing. May seemed to think that we came from a very grand family (at that time my father was working hard to set up his own business again and the reality was that we were not very well off) and Sunday lunch was an eye opener to me. I could never remember having a main meal where as well as potatoes we had *two* vegetables. It certainly impressed me. After lunch May had to go and open the pub and Dad and I took Doreen for a walk in her pram.

45

May's parents were a wizened little couple; her father sat huddled in a corner of the bar and drank the profits, while her mother hovered anxiously in the background. It was obvious that it was May who ran the pub although her father was the tenant. Eventually we left and drove home and neither then or at any other time did Auntie Ethel ever ask me where I went with my father on a regular basis.

It was many years before I was able to appreciate the dilemma my father found himself in. Struggling to set up his business, he lived in his sister's house and to that extent he was her only support. His own house was let to tenants whom the law of the land at that time prevented him from evicting, even though they gave endless trouble over paying their rent. May, in any event, was married, and she refused to attempt a divorce which she could in all probability have got on the grounds of desertion. Again her sentimentality came to bear, as she told me she didn't want my father's name to appear in the papers. I continued to visit there and sometimes stayed over a weekend. On one occasion, a man May's family knew asked to take me to the pictures. He had lost a leg in the war and I felt a bit sorry for him, so I went, but when he brought me back to the house, when May was in the pub, he tried to force me to kiss me. His mouth was all wet and slobbery and I fought him off and fled to my room. I avoided him from then on. It was May's brother Billy, who showed me the photos of Belsen and who confided in me that he was having an affair.

Meanwhile, my father had obtained three second-hand trucks 'on the never-never', as he put it, and employed three drivers. He spent his time touring the builders to find work, sometimes driving a truck himself if one of the men failed to turn up and doing his own repairs in the area he had from Auntie Maryon off Benton Bank and under the bridge. In the evenings, from time to time, he would have me help him with the accounts and to type his business letters on the old 'sit-up-and-beg' typewriter. As I struggled with invoice layouts and messy carbon paper, I invented my own hit-and-miss way of typing, which I do to this day, with some speed but not much accuracy. One night we were totting up columns of figures at the dining-room table when I suddenly found myself in the grip of hysterical laughter at the way my father moved his pen on the paper. My father must have realised he had pushed me too far and I was allowed to go to bed early with a hot drink.

I can't remember how I found out about youth hostelling, but it inspired my interest and I managed to pursuade my cousin Sheila from North Shields to come with me. Sheila was supposed to have been born with some heart defect, but walking was something she was encouraged to do and so we kitted ourselves out. Army surplus was in its heyday so we bought army capes against the weather, substantial shoes – I was never able to afford proper boots, but nailed studs into the soles of my shoes – rucksacks and warm socks. One joined the Association and was given details of the available hostels and a card that would be stamped at each hostel visited. We would go at the weekend as Sheila was working by then, and we would catch a bus from Newcastle in the direction we were going on the Friday evening making sure that we only had a short walk to the hostel. They were pretty basic, some with a few more amenities than others, but usually there was a dormitory with bunks for girls and another for boys. The kitchen would hold a long bench with a range of gas rings using bottled gas and the toilets were generally outdoors and of the privy kind. Early next morning we would set off, I with my compass and inch-to-the-mile map, and make our way to the next hostel; sometimes this would be across the moors or perhaps along country lanes. Occasionally we would be offered a lift, which we never turned down, as it took some time for our feet to harden and initially we would be plagued with blisters.

47

On one occasion we had stayed on the Friday at a hostel on the Roman wall and when we set off the next morning there was a heavy mist. We struck off up to the moors following sheep tracks and as we breasted a slope beyond which was a small tarn, suddenly the mist cleared, and as the tarn came into view a flight of geese took off from the water and disappeared into the remaining mist on the other side of the lake. Magical! Often in the autumn there would be mushrooms to collect along the way and we would stop at lunchtime, light a fire and cook them in the open. Sometimes it poured with rain and we would put on our capes, and with heads down push on as best we could. It was a great training ground for learning perseverance.

At school I struggled on attempting to catch up, but my heart wasn't really in it. I was once commended for an essay I had written and was asked to read it out in class. The subject was 'Windows' and I visualised a room with three windows. Out of the first there was life as we knew it, out of the second was destruction and despair, and out of the third a present-day Adam and Eve rose out of the ruins to face the brave new world. No doubt this was the outcome of all we had experienced over the last few years. I was asked by the same teacher what I thought of Virginia Woolf when she came across me reading one of her books. I had to tell her that in all truth, the answer was 'not very much'. The book, I think, was *To the Lighthouse*, which dispensed with capital letters and sentence construction, which offended my sense of order.

I had been sent to take piano lessons again at one point, but really couldn't stand them. As it was with our family, I made no objection but just stopped going, although I would leave the house with my music portfolio. After some time I put in an appearance again and found someone else at my lesson. Of course my father must have been informed, but no one ever said anything. However, I loved music and when there was a concert on the radio I would sit with my ear glued to it as, although it was never turned off, it was played very softly in our house. Seeing my interest, Sheila's elder sister Marian and her husband Marshall, an art teacher, once took me to a concert at the City Hall. It was rather distracting to actually see the instruments performing rather than just absorbing the music, a bit off-putting somehow.

I should explain here the various pronunciations of the name 'Marian' which so often cropped up in our family. I don't really know if there are different spellings, but Auntie Maryon, Ethel's sister, was Maryon, as was Sheila's sister, but my cousin was Marian as in Maid Marian. Very confusing.

I enjoyed the science subjects at school and did quite well at biology, chemistry and physics; English literature and language was OK, but French was a complete non-starter. Maths began quite well until we ran into algebra, which made no sense at all to me, while geometry had been fine until we reached Pythagoras, at which point my interest waned. All too soon, the School Certificate exam loomed. My friends Jean Alison and Stella Ritchie were already in the sixth form, when I realised I would have to pull my socks up and do some studying. Now that I had my own bedroom, I would sit at the windowsill as the evenings grew darker with a table lamp beside me and do as much revision as I could. It paid off as I passed my exams and even managed to collect a few credits. The problem was what to do next. My father couldn't afford for me to stay on into the sixth form, even if I had been considered capable of the additional work. We went to consult a careers expert where I wasn't a great deal of help. I would have liked to be an architect but my maths was hopeless. My father had been quite ill as a boy and had spent a lot of time in hospital. Consequently, he greatly admired the nursing profession, and so, although I had never seen the inside of a hospital in my life, it was decided that that was what I would do. However,

49

there was one snag as I was only 17 and I needed to be 18 before I would be accepted. I would have liked to have spent the year as a nursery nurse, but neither Dad nor the careers lady thought that was a good idea, so it was decided that I would do a year's pre-nursing course at Rutherford College, an all-girls' school on the other side of town.

Once I was 17 my father said he would send me for driving lessons. We applied for my provisional licence and he said that once I had learned the basics at the school, he would complete my tuition. My cousin Marian, who was four months older than me, had already got her provisional licence, but her impatient and, it has to be said, arrogant, father decided to teach her himself. It was a complete disaster given her nervous disposition, and although in later years she did learn to drive, she was never confident and gave up after having an minor accident some years later. I passed my test first time round with a great sense of achievement.

Auntie Ethel, who had been employed by the post office during and just after the war, was now made redundant as the men returned home to take up their jobs. So she began to do more for the WVS. Once I had my driving licence I would occasionally be roped in to drive the dilapidated Meals on Wheels van round the Shieldfield area of Newcastle. It was quite an eye opener to take the hot meals in to some of the more deprived houses, where, as often as not, it was the smell that met you first. But on the whole they were glad of the help and would proudly produce an immaculately cleaned plate to return from the last meal to be delivered. Other jobs were found for me during school holidays; one poor man had lost his wife, whether by death or desertion I never knew, but there was a gap in his child care between the regular helper leaving and his arrival home from work which I was asked to fill. There were three young children and I would see that they ate the tea the minder had left for them and amuse them until their father came home.

50

Another lady who lived in Jesmond was confined to bed for some reason. Her bed was in the downstairs front room and raised up high so that she could see out of the window. She also had a three-month-old baby and I would be asked to go and baby-sit for an hour or two while her mother, a patrician-like lady with a wealth of well-controlled white hair, went to do some shopping or to take a break. Another job which I rather enjoyed was baby-sitting for some of the upwardly mobile of Jesmond. I would arrive to find them in evening dress all ready for some formal occasion or for a visit to the theatre. The children were generally already tucked up in bed but I would be introduced. They usually left me a meal in the oven to have at my leisure and I would settle in front of the fire with a good book. The man of the house would drive me home afterwards and I would receive half-a-crown for myself. So in those years, I saw a great cross section of need and of social circumstances in the city.

At the end of the year's pre-nursing course I took the first part of my nursing preliminary exams. It had been an interesting course in which, as well as anatomy and physiology, I had learned hygiene and invalid cookery. That was a laugh – I even had a certificate to prove it. Our group also visited places like the sewage works and the waste disposal depot, although we never came anywhere near a hospital. The other girls on the course were going to various hospitals and I was the only one going to the General. Suddenly school was over and life was beckoning.

5

Exams finished in June and then there was an interview with one of the assistant matrons at the general hospital prior to acceptance. I don't feel that I put up a very good show; I had no idea what I would be asked about and when questioned about my hobbies I said very little about my various activities as I thought they meant things like needlework, painting or perhaps a little woodcarving. And when it came to saying why I wanted to be a nurse, I expect I was completely tongue-tied as I really had no idea and certainly no sense of vocation. I could hardly say my dad thought it would be a good idea. Well, I guess they must have been desperate for staff as I was accepted and some time later I presented myself at the hospital linen room, a vast area and hive of activity, where with several others I was measured for my uniform.

Student nurses were accepted in batches every three months and in the summer of 1948 the National Health Service had been born. I don't recall being aware of that fact, or if I was, whether it would have any impact on my future. I dare say that when our clutch of hopefuls presented ourselves in September of that year, not a great deal had changed. Our first task was to go to the linen room again and be issued with the uniforms for which we had been measured. These consisted of three stiff cotton blue-and-white-striped dresses with short sleeves and without a collar. The collars came ready-shaped in some stiff white material like the gentlemen's collars of that time which were rapidly going out of fashion. I was used to my father wearing his, and with the collar studs which impaled them to the dress at the throat. We each had a set of white aprons the bib of which fitted under the collar with two strips over the shoulders, crossed over the shoulder blades at the back then brought round and tied under the bust. The waistband was then fitted around the waist and fastened at the back in a series of contortions with two more collar studs. Somewhat bemused, we were given several white starched oblong squares which were to be our caps, followed by a crash course on how to prepare them. With experience we learned to make our caps last for several days and to have them ready the night before to slap on in the morning hustle of preparation. I will explain, but unless you can see one being done, it may be hard to visualise. First of all, it was necessary to be seated, then one long side of the material was folded back and forward on itself to form a firm base; this was then stretched around the slightly raised knee while at the same time, the softer inner material was gathered up into folds. When both hands met with the folded material, a large safety pin was pushed through all the layers to produce a shape which would perch upon the head. One was left with the other long side of material dangling uselessly down, but it was then lifted up and folded over the top of the cap to form a 'tail' and the two points at the bottom were secured with a further safety pin. This was a 'taily cap', and was secured to the head with a hair slide on each side of the head. (At that time hair clips did not have their ends protected with a rubber cover, and most nurses I knew, myself included, ended up with damaged front teeth from opening up the hair clips.) Best of all, however, were our cloaks. Made of heavy navy blue wool with hoods and a red wool lining, they settled over our shoulders and were held in place by crossed-over belts attached at the shoulders.

We also had an outdoor uniform but this was provided by ourselves. It consisted of a navy blue gabardine raincoat and a round hat of the same material. Shoes of course were black, low and comfortable and we wore black stockings. This was when nylons were still not readily available and when they were, were too expensive for us. Our stockings were lisle in winter and silk in summer with a tendency to ladder. Much time was spent repairing ladders with a cute little piece of equipment which would weave the run back up the leg. Holes in the heels and toes were harder to fix, but we soon discovered that a strip of plaster camouflaged with black ink would extend the life of most stockings.

Still not having been anywhere near a hospital ward, we were sent off to Close House, a beautiful Georgian house near Heddon-on-the-Wall to the west of Newcastle. It stood in large grounds on a slope overlooking the Tyne Valley, and being somewhat off the beaten track, its remoteness made for few distractions. We soon made the most of what distractions there were. We were assigned to our rooms and five of us were allocated a lovely large room spartanly furnished with an iron bedstead each, a locker and a small bedside rug on the polished wood floor. Bedding was scant and as the autumn frosts descended, we put the rugs over our beds to keep warm. We thought this was a huge joke, but someone's parent must have complained, for we were later issued with another blanket each.

On the ground floor we had a classroom and a room where we learned practical matters such as bed making, bed bathing and tray and trolley setting. Whatever the function, there was the requisite tray or trolley to be set 'just so' and they had to be learned by heart. Before classes began we each had our morning duties which were delegated by the two sister-tutors in charge. We cleaned the rooms and the stairs, the bathrooms and toilets but not the kitchens. The most hated duty was setting the breakfast table for the sisters. Instructions were given once only and expected to be memorised. Each plate, each knife, the butter dish, the marmalade pot, the cups and saucers, the teapot stand and tea cosy, the toast rack, the napkins and their holders, all had to be placed exactly in position. Inspection did not take place then. One finished the task and went to have breakfast in the common dining room. But then would come the dreaded summons. In front of everyone else the call would come to return to the sisters' private dining room and to be given a dressing down if everything was not in its appointed place. I probably got called back more than anyone else to that hated task.

We started on our anatomy and physiology course assisted by the resident skeleton called Horace whose bony protuberances and joints had to be memorised along with the intricacies of the bones of the inner ear, the structure of the skull and the complex 'putting together' of the pelvis.

Evenings were spent revising our notes but it didn't take us too long to find the road to the nearest village with a pub, the Three Tuns, at Heddon-on-the-Wall. Never having been in a pub before except at the other side of the counter in May's pub in Alnick, it didn't take me long to appreciate the joy of a glass of cider. The pub was on the primitive side and the lavatories were in the form of a detached stone building on the other side of the yard, where, on entering it was necessary to climb a wide step to reach the two-seater wood plank stretched over the midden which exuded a strong smell and a fierce breeze to freeze the nether parts. Overcome with giggles at this arrangement, Dorothy lost her balance and twisted her ankle as she stumbled on the step and we had to assist her back to base with many injunctions to silence as we stifled our giggles.

We always seemed to be hungry and it wasn't long before we discovered that a path in the other direction from the pub led across several fields and across the Military Road (no doubt named for the Romans who built it) to a wooden shack were we could buy a meal of ham, egg and chips.

One night, as we returned from a more innocent stroll in the grounds, we approached the house, now silhouetted against the rosy aftermath of the setting sun across the valley towards the west. There was a hard frost and the ground sparkled in the last of the dying light while above and behind us the stars began to stab the deep navy blue of the oncoming night sky. From the house came the tinkling sounds of Mendelssohn played by Mary Swain on the elderly piano left by the owners of the house. Mary, one of our number, was often to give us great pleasure by her playing, both here and later at the Nurses' Home on Westgate Road.

My roommates were to become fast friends. Dorothy Waters was in her early twenties and therefore somewhat older than the rest of us. It was a lifetime ambition of hers to become a nurse and having left school at fourteen she had worked in several jobs before she succeeded in gaining a place on the training programme. Jean Clayton was my age, the younger child of older parents who lived at Wylam. Her much older brother, Ossie Clayton, was a friend of my Uncle Harry. Both Jean and Dorothy were beanpole thin and wiry while Doreen Wilkinson was a larger build. She was somewhat retiring but with a calm nature, and we never really knew much about Doreen's private life. Joan Carroll, also a larger lady, came from Middlesbrough where her father was in the police force. It was many years later that I realised Joan was of mixed race; she had taken us to her home and her mother, of a darker hue, was very upset and mortified that she had invited us. We found it hard to understand as Joan was our dear friend and it mattered not to us where her mother may have originated, but it was my first encounter with the ramifications of race relations. Her mother must have suffered rejection in one form or another and assumed that when Joan's friends found out the truth we would despise her.

The three months seemed to drag and we were all eager for them to end and for our lives on the wards to commence. While we were there the Cold War began. In the post-war negotiations between the victorious nations, the Russian 'Niet' became an ongoing chorus as they used their veto to undermine the search for a lasting peace, and it became evident that our erstwhile allies were no longer our friends. Uncle Joe Stalin was obviously not the jolly, kind gentleman we had thought him to be; in fact in no time at all the Iron Curtain of Churchill's description came down and we feared that another war was inevitable with the added worry of nuclear capability. For us, a generation with first-hand experience of bombers flying overhead with their deadly cargoes, and with the added fear of the carnage one nuclear bomb could wreak upon a city, this was no laughing matter. We felt that before long a state of emergency would be called and we would leave our haven in the country to take up duties in the hospital. But the nations pulled back from confrontation, our three months were concluded and we were taken by bus back to Newcastle and deposited at the door of the nurses' home across the road from the hospital on Westgate Road.

Here, Home Sister allocated us our rooms, mostly single rooms with a built-in wardrobe, a bed and a bedside locker, with bathrooms and toilets at the end of the wide central highly polished corridor. The ground floor held the kitchens and dining room and a large lounge with comfortable sofas which was hardly ever used, except when Mary Swain played the piano. Additionally, for the first month we had to attend PE lessons in the morning, to limber us up for the onslaught ahead, I expect.

Across the road, the part of the hospital fronting the road was the old workhouse built of stone blocks. Behind that were a series of two-storey nineteenth-century wards round three sides of a square. These were used for purely medical cases while behind them were buildings housing casualty, outpatients, the dispensary and office buildings. Off on the right were other older buildings; those nearest the road held a couple of small wards for acute mental patients, while further along were classrooms. Then behind all this was a wide area of gardens and lawns before coming to the front of the newer buildings where a long corridor stretched back with spurs off for a variety of wards, mostly surgical, with the operating theatres half way down and that very special hushed area where Matron and her two assistant matrons held sway.

Dorothy, Jean and I were allocated to the children's ward half way down the long corridor of the newer building, where we presented ourselves promptly at 7 a.m. to Sister Palfreyman, who was expecting us. We tried to make ourselves as inconspicuous as possible in Sister's office as the routine of the morning handover from the night staff took place. In the ward report book every patient was listed with their treatment and their ongoing condition and at the end it was duly signed by the night nurse in charge and then by the day staff. Off went the night staff to their beds and the morning duties were then allocated by Sister. Dorothy and Jean went off to the large ward at the end of the spur while I was handed over to a middle-aged 'seen-it-all' assistant nurse who led me in to a large side ward holding five metal cots set against the walls. Each cot contained a toddler of two to three years of age, all of whom I was told were suffering from TB meningitis. In one cot, the little girl had soiled herself, and her night clothes, her bedding and most of the cot sides were well smeared. My first task was to clean it up. Not having had younger brothers and sisters I had no idea where to start, but I was taken to the sluice room where we set a trolley with a bowl of warm water, cloths, cotton wool and Dettol and then collected clean linen from the linen room. Gently we washed the little mite who, because of her condition, found every touch painful. My teacher then took pity on me and let me sit in a low chair and nurse the little girl as she cleaned up the rest of the cot. The child's name was Louise and sadly she died a few weeks later. We carefully laid her out in the day room at the end of the ward and surrounded her with flowers as her parents came to see her. Benny, a lively little boy, had a shunt in his skull through which he was given some of the precious new drug, penicillin, but either his treatment or his disease had caused him to lose the use of one arm and leg. However, once let out of the cot, he could shuffle along at a rate of knots.

There were also a few smaller private rooms for children or small babies needing special attention and I was shown how to tape a test tube to the penis of a baby boy in order to collect a urine specimen. A few days later I was told to collect a specimen from the baby in the next room. In I trotted with my test tube at the ready only to find it was a baby girl. There were howls of mirth from the staff nurse when she later discovered I had carefully – and hopefully – propped the test tube up against the child. My own common sense should have told me that a kidney dish should have been the implement of choice!

The children in the larger ward were mostly medical cases, one with cystic fibrosis, a young girl of about twelve who had to be bent over a wooden 'horse' on her bed while her back was soundly thumped to help clear her lungs. It seems that is one treatment that has stayed the same. One non-medical case was a young ten-year-old tearaway who, while playing with friends near the electric railway line, had fallen and severely burnt his skull. Not even that stopped his mischief, however.

Visiting was confined to parents only and was allowed twice a week on Wednesday and Sunday afternoons. One of us would be delegated to stand at the door with a trolley and collect and label all the 'goodies' that the loving parents brought in for their children, and later it was up to Sister as to who got what.

The weekly work schedules were prepared by Sister, so of course she and Staff Nurse took turns to have Saturday and Sundays off. Our hours were from 7 a.m. to 7 p.m., and

59

with luck we might have three evenings off, one immediately preceding our one day off. Mornings off were popular as there was the chance of a lie in, but once a week we each had the dreaded split shift where we worked in the morning, had a few hours off in the afternoon, then returned to work in the evening. For the first few months our pay was a £1 per month, but then, probably for the one and only time in its history, the National Health Service doubled our pay and we received £2 a month. This we were told we were to consider as pocket money, and indeed we did as we had our accommodation, our food, our uniforms and our laundry provided for us, but we were always hard up as we had to buy our text books which were expensive hard backs in the days before paperbacks were printed. But 10 shillings a week went a long way in days when a large loaf of bread cost 4d and tram fares were at the most, 2d or 3d. Sometimes the management of the town cinemas would leave tickets at the nurses' home for morning trade shows, but we often queued for the 'gods' and went to see the ballet, the opera and D'Oyly Carte as they came to town.

As a spin off from my youth hostelling, I had joined up with a group who went country dancing at the White City at Whitley Bay, where we danced the Eightsome Reel, the Flowers of Edinburgh, the Strathspey, and other favourites to the music of Jimmy Shand and his band. Rose's father farmed some land just north of Whitley Bay and on one splendid occasion we held a dance in the barn her father had had newly floored. I had a boyfriend, Jim, who was a miner, very handsome, and I was the envy of all the girls. He came hiking with Sheila and me and sometimes Rose came too. Once when I had a weekend off, we hiked through Staward Peel, where we built a fire in the woods and cooked our lunch.

Jim was not my first boyfriend; when I was sixteen, Brian was a tall sixth-former who attended Heaton Secondary

School. He was a good-looking red-headed lad and on school mornings he would walk down from his house at the top of the hill on the Jesmond side and we would stand and talk until my tram arrived to take me to school. I dare say we made a very striking pair in our smart school uniforms, mine brown and his navy blue. He was a friend of my cousin Philip who lived next door to us and who would often join us on our long Sunday walks through Jesmond Dene. Brian was an only child, when, no doubt to the consternation of his parents, his mother gave birth to twin girls. Our Sunday walks then attracted quite a lot of attention as we wheeled the twin pram along the wide crowded pathways among the Sunday strollers in the days before gymslip mums became something of a commonplace. Then there was Mike, who was somewhat older than me. He picked me up in Newcastle one Saturday and I went out with him for quite a while. There were several others whose names I no longer remember, but I was seldom without a boyfriend. It used to puzzle me as to how you would know when *the* one came along, because, although I always started out quite liking them, after a few weeks, well three months at the most, I lost interest and gave them the order of the boot.

However, Jim lasted for quite a while as we had much in common. He was ambitious and was studying to become an overseer at the mine. One weekend, when the mine was closed down, he obtained permission to take me underground to see the workings. It was quite eerie to go below in the cage and to walk along the silent galleries. The thing that I remember most was the pervading smell of damp earth and the claustrophobic knowledge of being so far below the surface.

Now that I had so much less spare time to spend at home, my work for my father was limited to preparing the wages of the lorry drivers. I did not go to Alnwick so often either, but one night when I was at home alone, the phone went

61

and a wavering voice which I recognised as May's mother asked me to tell my father that May was ill, and could he come. He left later that night and I was not to know what had happened until I next went to Alnwick with Dad. There May gave me a blow by blow account of how she had given birth to a son at home. In her panic the child had been born into a chamber pot where he had died. I had not known she was pregnant again, not having been there for some time, but I had nightmares about that poor little baby who would have been my father's only son.

Needless to say, I was unable to confide this to anyone, even less my friends, as Jean's brother, being a friend of Uncle Harry, would have been a direct link back to the family, so to this day, no one else in the family ever knew, and really, May had no business to tell me, young girl that I was.

The next ward I went on was for a three-month stint on the men's surgical ward. It was believed at that time that flowers should be removed from the wards at night as they used up precious oxygen in the air, so the final job before going off duty was to go round with a trolley, collect them all up and take them to the day room. Next morning, the fun began as we attempted to sort out whose belonged to whom. I hated flowers, especially when the visitors arrived with unwieldy bunches which we were expected to take and somehow find vases to fit them into. I never became enamoured of flower arranging. Our main task as probationers was to do the beds and backs each morning. Surgical patients at that time were not encouraged to get out of bed, and so washing water, bottles and bedpans, as well as regular meals, all had to be brought to each patient. The wards did not have curtains around the beds; instead, we had to manoeuvre curtained screens on wheels up and down the wards whenever privacy was needed. The bed trolley, laden with sheets and pillowcases from the linen cupboard on the lower shelf, and a bowl, washcloth, soap, surgical spirit and talcum powder on the upper one, was lugged from bed to bed along with the receptacle for soiled linen. Two chairs would be set at the end of the bed and the bedclothes would be folded and lifted on to the chairs until only the sheet remained to cover the patient. After a quick wash, the area at the base of the spine would be vigorously rubbed with moist soap until it was absorbed. Then the same area was rubbed with surgical spirit until dry and then smoothed with talcum powder. This was to prevent bedsores, the scourge of the bed-bound patient. The draw sheet would then be pulled through to give a cool, smooth bit to sit on, the pillows plumped up and, where needed, a 'donkey' placed under the knees to keep the patient upright. This was a bolster wrapped in a draw sheet and tucked under the bed. Then all the bedclothes went back on, renewed with clean ones where necessary. Top sheet and top blanket were folded back at the bottom to give easy access for the surgeons and the quilts were given precise hospital corners so that when looking down the ward, Sister could see a well turned-out row of beds. This task usually took all morning, in between taking four-hourly temperatures and pulses of everyone and entering them in the book, and blood pressures where necessary.

Staff Nurse would do the dressings. Every night the autoclaves in the bowels of the hospital would sterilise drums of dressings which were delivered next morning to the treatment room on the ward. Trolley setting was an art; the whole upper shelf was washed down with Dettol and then one of the sterilised drums would be opened and with the aid of a pair of Spencer Wells forceps, a cloth the size of a tea towel would be taken out and laid across it. From the bubbling steriliser in the corner would come stainless steel galley pots and kidney bowls which would contain iodine, mercurochrome, cotton wool and gauze swabs, followed by scissors, forceps and probes. All would then be covered by another sterilised cloth. We were given turns at assisting with the dressings, and we also learned how to give enemas and stomach washouts, both unpleasant procedures for us and for the patients. Operating days were hectic, but if we were off duty, we could see what the operating list was, and if there was anything interesting we could ask permission of Theatre Sister and go and watch.

Christmas at the hospital was a very special time. On the surgical wards, the operating list was curtailed, and on the other wards, every patient who could be was discharged home before the holidays. For weeks beforehand, each ward decided upon its theme for the Christmas decorations, when the huge medicine cabinets in the centre of the ward would be turned into a scene from a nursery rhyme, a pantomime or a Disney story. At that time we had only seen *Bambi* and *Snow White and the Seven Dwarfs*, but there was much fertile ground for inspiration there. Papier-mâché figures were made and decorations fashioned with the aid of many rolls of cotton wool. On Christmas Eve, myself and a group of nurses warmly wrapped in our cloaks and carrying lanterns strolled the grounds, the corridors and the stairs singing carols, while on Christmas Day itself, with fewer patients and a full complement of nurses, we soon made the beds, took the temperatures, administered the medicines and the injections and did any necessary dressings. Then we were free to take our turns visiting the others wards and admiring their decorations, kept under wraps until then. Ward sisters were judged by their largesse to their staff, and dishes of nuts and sweets and bowls of tangerines and apples were to be had. In turns, we went to the various sittings of splendid Christmas lunches and the afternoon was spent in a state of torpor as the doors were opened to as many visitors as the patients cared to have.

We continued with our lectures, which had to be squeezed in alongside our other duties, and at that time of 1948 to

1949, when penicillin was still not readily available to the population as a whole, one of our lectures was on the management of pneumonia, with its periods of crisis, its rust-coloured sputum and the necessity to sponge the patient regularly. I never saw a case of pneumonia, I am happy to say, but it must have been a very traumatic illness. We were also taught how to make poultices of mustard, linseed and even bread, but antiflogistine was the preferred sticky method. I never had to use those either, but our sister-tutors were obviously having a hard time catching up with more modern ideas. They certainly never let up on the stern inflexibility towards us!

The lecture which provoked most mirth was in the hygiene course where we had to learn about fleas, bed bugs and head lice. In no time at all, we were all surreptitiously scratching at our heads or our persons.

One day, at the nurses' home, one of the girls in our group, a rather strange-looking girl who puzzled us all, beckoned me off the corridor into her room. Whispering urgently, she pulled me over to one side of the window and, peering carefully out, she said to me, 'Can you see them down there?' 'Who?' I asked. 'Those men at the corner,' she said.

Hard as I looked, I could see no one at all, let alone anyone looking suspicious. I told her as much, but she was insistent and said that she was being followed and that 'they' knew where she was. Somewhat alarmed, I sought out Home Sister and told her what had happened; she told me not to worry and that she would see to it. Poor girl, next day her belongings had gone and her room was empty. We could only think that she must have been suffering from some sort of breakdown.

My first tour of night duty was during the summer months and was on one of the male medical wards. These wards were situated on three sides of the large square behind the old workhouse buildings. The central doorway and staircase opened up onto two floors of wards, one to the right and one to the left. At the apex of the far corners was another staircase with, at right angles, a further two wards, one on each level. Being medical wards they were deemed not to need such a concentration of staff, so that two wards in each spur were run as one, with Sister's office at each corner. The night staff came on and the report was read out by the departing day staff and two, or at the most three, of us would be in charge of the ward for the night. The patients would be settled down with hot drinks, the last round of temperature taking and dispensing of medicines. Very ill patients might be 'specialed', with one of us sitting by the bedside all night, but generally nights were quiet and I took up embroidery to pass the time. After a hot day, the large windows would be raised to let in the cool air, and in that part of the hemisphere, often the light never completely left the sky between the lingering sunset and the early dawn. In the gardens below were planted night-scented stocks whose perfume had no trouble in overcoming the hospital smells. We were allowed a long meal break half way through the night and we would repair to the canteen where we joined in raucous songs accompanied by clacking spoons held between the fingers.

Night Sister's rounds were made from time to time, and the first task on moving to a new ward was to learn the name, diagnosis and treatment of each of fifty-odd patients by heart. Should you have been left in charge of the ward when she arrived, then it was your duty to accompany her with her torch to each bed and recite each patient's history and answer any questions she may ask.

On night duty we worked on a fortnightly basis, with ten nights on and four off and instead of sleeping in the noisy nurses' home, we had rooms in a large Victorian house in the next street where silence all day was a requirement. And so on a sunny June morning I would reach my room, close

66

the rose-coloured curtains and sink into a dreamless sleep. I would go home to Woodburn on my nights off, arriving in the morning and going straight to bed. I would sleep all day, get up for a meal, sleep all night, and if not aroused, sleep for most of the next morning. I loved night duty; it was not so physically onerous but in addition there was a feeling of living on a different level to the rest of humanity. While they slept, a whole different life went on, and the day-to-day business of ordinary affairs passed us by.

One night when I came on duty we had a new patient called Charlie who soon became a firm favourite of us all. In his late thirties or thereabouts, he was a fireman and he was suffering from coronary thrombosis. As I did my rounds on the second night he was in, he asked me to light him a cigarette as he was not allowed to do anything for himself. I took the cigarette from the packet and placed it in his mouth, then struck the match to light it. As he took the first drag upon it, he suddenly fell back on the pillow, the cigarette dropped to the floor, and to my horror, he was dead. We put the screens around his bed and called Night Sister, who certified his death, and then we had the task of laying him out.

Looking back, it must seem heartless, but if we knew a patient was dying, we hoped and prayed it would be after we had gone off duty, because even if it was only five minutes before we were due to go, we would have to stay and do the laying out. This was always done with great respect and the body was prepared in the best possible way and gently dressed in the paper-like laying-out gown and wrapped in a sheet before calling the porters for it to be taken on a trolley with a rounded cover to the morgue at the back of the hospital.

All of this made a social life a bit difficult. I still managed to see Stella for occasional Monday night visits to the Playhouse, but Jean Allison, my other school friend, and I had lost touch. When we were about 15 Jean's mother died of cancer and it was not very long after that that her father, a Methodist minister, married one of the ladies from his church. Jean and her sisters were very fond of her, but I would guess that there was some talk in the church on Northumberland Road. Anyhow, her father was moved to a church in Leeds, where I went to stay for a holiday at the large old Victorian terrace house in Roundhay. I was made very welcome and Jean and I enjoyed our holiday, the highlight being a visit to Harrogate with tea at Betty's famous cafe. But it seemed that our paths were to divide and I gradually lost touch with her.

There were several male nurses training at the hospital and one I quite fancied was an Irishman called Tommy O'Neill. He was a Catholic and when I told my dad about him he was a bit worried. As he said, don't get too serious – in marriage there are enough things to argue about without having a ready-made excuse. He had very little time for the Church, and who could blame him? When my mother died so young at 29, the local priest visited the grieving young man and accused him of causing her death because he had taken her away from the Church. I expect he was referring to the fact that my mother was a lapsed Catholic and had not received the last rites, and in his opinion, would therefore be in purgatory. At least I think that is how it goes, but really, that was hardly the thing to fling at my father at that time. Suffice to say, my father was concerned, but he had no need to worry. Tommy, charming and humorous though he was, was great company and fun to be with, but was not the love of my life. He did impinge on it somewhat, however, as I was supposedly still going out with Jim at that time, so one night I was escorted back to Woodburn by Tommy, with much giggling on the doorstep, only to find as I let myself in that Jim had spent the evening at our house in the company of a very embarrassed Auntie Ethel, waiting for me to come home. I must have appeared with flushed face and smudged lipstick as that was the end of Jim and me, but I didn't really care as I was finding him a bit boring and there was so much more going on in my life.

Of course, although we could not begin nursing training until we were 18, at that time the 'coming of age' was still not until 21, so the hospital matron and sisters took their duties *in loco parentis* very seriously. The door to the right in the entrance hall of the nurses' home led to a bare room with a table and chair, and on the table was The Book. Any nurse returning to the Home after 10 p.m. was required to sign her name and the time that she returned. The next morning the book went to Matron and if too many late nights were recorded, a severe lecture was on the cards. However, it was an unwritten rule that the first one back after 10 p.m., no matter what the time was, would write down, say, 10.02. The next one would write perhaps 10.05 then perhaps a flurry at 10.10. Provided no goody-goody put the correct time in it was possible to come back at 11 p.m. and be signed in for 10.15. However, if a *really* late night was needed for a bit of serious courting, all was not lost. All that was needed was a mate who would leave the downstairs cloakroom window open, and for a boyfriend strong enough and with nerves of steel who could bunk you in through the window.

My next ward was the neurosurgical ward where patients were recovering from operations for such serious conditions as brain tumours and back operations for slipped discs. As more intense nursing was required there were fewer beds and the work was not so heavy as on the medical wards. Later I did a stint on the neurosurgical theatre where I learned to operate the diathermy machine and to hold the head of a patient steady as the surgeon used his carpenter-like tools of drills and bits to remove a circle of bone to relieve pressure or to cut a larger piece to operate on a tumour. One favourite operation for someone suffering with back problems was called manipulation and was done under a general anaesthetic. I sometimes wondered if the patient ever realised that one of the porters was called in to do the heavy work of bending and stretching the spine!

Perhaps because of my experience on the neurosurgical side, the next time I was on night duty I was asked by Night Sister if I would undertake 'specialing' of three patients who had been operated on, more or less as an experiment, by severing the frontal lobes of their brains from the remainder. It was called a frontal lobotomy, and had been performed on three very violent mental patients, and for that reason they were to be nursed in a top room on the block just inside the front gate of the hospital which was allocated to mental patients. On the ground floor there were three padded cells where violent women were kept for emergency assessment. The next floor held classrooms and was empty through the night, and my patients were on the floor above. In low lights, through the nights I regularly monitored their vital signs, with an occasional visit from Night Sister, and a meal half way through when I was relieved by one of the mental nurses from below. In the morning, before I left, I would assist with breakfasts for the poor demented souls on the ground floor.

My next ward was on the female medical ward, where in a side ward we had a young woman suffering from tuberculosis. She was thin and emaciated and it was my job to give her injections of streptomycin into her poor leg. Her skin was toughened and there was very little muscle to inject into. It was so painful and she would cry and I would hold her to comfort her. Perhaps I shouldn't have done so.

One duty that I disliked intensely was a short two weeks filling in on the private wards. I was to take the place of a nurse who was suffering from TB. Catherine had gloriously thick red hair which she struggled to keep in check beneath her cap. But when I saw her later after several months of illness it had faded to a speckled straw colour, as indeed she herself had faded. We were all given tests which supposedly showed whether we were likely to be resistant to TB or not, but obviously these were not infallible. So I was sent to take her place for a couple of weeks until other arrangements could be made, but they were two of the worst weeks of my life. The women in the private rooms, most of whom had had some sort of surgery, were petty and demanding. It seemed that having paid their way, they felt they could treat us as menials, even though we did not receive extra pay for their care. The lights above their doors would be forever flashing as they demanded windows open, windows closed, flowers arranged, water jugs refilled, anything and everything but nursing care. So I was relieved when I left that ward and swore I would never become a nurse in a private nursing home. My sights were set on completing my training and obtaining my SRN qualifications, and then perhaps to do a midwifery course. After that there were many options and I saw an interesting career stretching ahead of me.

Jean and I had attended a lecture at the City Hall held by a medical missionary in Africa and when the collection plate came around, so impressed was I, that I put in a 10-shilling note, a very large bite out of my small income. After the talk when the missionary asked for volunteers to help him with the work, Jean and I went backstage to meet him and said that once our training was over we would love to do such worthwhile work.

Some weeks later, on the neurosurgical ward, an outgoing patient left money to be distributed among the staff. My share was 10 shillings. The question was, was my generosity being rewarded, or, on the other hand, was it not required?

My second bout of night duty approached, as did my twentieth birthday. I had almost completed my second year of nursing, had been left in charge of wards, was confident in my work, had many friends and a full life, but chance or fate, call it what you will, was to take a hand and my future was to change in so many ways and in so many more directions than I could ever have visualised.

6

Night duty was to be on the other male medical ward on the far side of the quadrangle. Meanwhile, lectures continued as we learned the signs and symptoms of various diseases and their treatments. The regular taking of temperatures was still a great part of nursing care, as infection was a spectre that haunted hospital wards. Antibiotics were still not generally available to the public at large and while we had the use of the sulphanilamides, penicillin was jealously guarded and only used in the most exceptional cases. It was only available in liquid form and was kept in the fridge, injections being given with well sterilised needles and syringes. Cleanliness on the wards was paramount and daily dusting of the lockers and the bedsteads with a damp duster was generally the first duty of a probationer nurse. Relaxations began to come through in the shape of ward assistants who took over the tasks of keeping water jugs filled and seeing to the dreaded flowers. Each ward had its own resident cleaner who lurked in the ward kitchen after the floors had been mopped and buffed to a high gloss. The cleaner also heated up the huge pans of coffee for the morning rounds, and on those awful days when the hospital kitchens were not able to send up a cooked breakfast, the cleaner would set a large pan of water to boil the enormous bowl of eggs that were supplied. It was then our job to rush around the ward dishing out the eggs, which usually meant that those served first got a half-raw egg while the last ones had a hard-boiled one. The main meals came from the kitchen in heated wheeled trolleys which were presided over by Sister as she dished out helpings

73

suitable to each patient. Special diets such as salt-free, milky or diabetic came up separately.

I was never to work on either the urology or the gynaecology ward, but when we met together we would have endless discussions about the patients that we had on our wards. One such woman had come in to the gynae ward for a hysterectomy after having a very large family. Her consultant felt that a further pregnancy would result in her death; however, it transpired that she was a Catholic and her priest arrived on the ward and persuaded her to discharge herself, no doubt to a certain death. We had long discussions on the question of which should be saved, a mother or a baby, in the event of it being impossible to save both, and we learned that in the Catholic philosophy, the child should be saved and the mother sacrificed. We were all also made very much aware that in the case of an impending death, the priest must be called post haste if the patient was Catholic, as failure to do so might result in that person's soul ending up in purgatory. It seemed a very harsh religion to me that could lay down such terrible rules, rules which I was sure were not called for in my own reading of the Bible.

At the end of the final chapter of our gynaecology text book we came across a passage that had us all rolling around with helpless laughter. It gave a list of foreign objects which from time to time had had to be extracted from the vagina by the medical profession. Among the articles was a jar a Vaseline but it concluded with the words, 'and a small bust of Napoleon' ...

As this was the early days of the National Health Service, we often saw patients whose health had been neglected due to lack of finance; enormous hernias were not uncommon, hopefully strapped up with stained leather trusses, but brought in as emergencies when strangulation took place. Dreadful uterine prolapses were often admitted which left me wondering how the poor souls had managed to walk with the protruding vagina between their legs. We had one poor man admitted who had fallen down the stairs at home and lain undiscovered for some days. We could see that even before the fall he had not been taking care of himself and it took much time and effort to peel off his stained and stiffened clothing and to clean his skin gently with paraffin oil to remove the caked filth before he could be washed.

I came onto the ward one night and went straight to Sister's office to hear the daytime report before having my duties allocated. A young man of 27 had been admitted through the day suffering from food poisoning but was stated to be in a stable condition. My job was to do the medicines and injections and when I came to the ward where he was, I found him sitting with some of the other men chatting comfortably. He seemed quite nice, with hazel eyes and Glenn Miller spectacles, about 5' 8" tall and stockily built. His smile was pleasant and he was obviously on good terms with all and sundry. I thought no more about him and continued my round. Next morning a fellow nurse, Jean Stirling, was quite excited about him as she said she knew him. He had been a Salvation Army officer, she said, which didn't mean a lot to me. I knew that there was a men's home near the hospital where tramps and down and outs stayed overnight, but I had no idea they were a religious group, as where we lived down Benton Bank we never saw their bands or their collectors. Jean was Scottish and liked to boast that she was Jean Stirling and she was born in Stirling Castle in Stirling and she spent as much time as she could hovering around the young man's bed. His name was Ronald Malone and he lived at the local Toc H club.

I came on duty the next night and he had been discharged, but as far as I was concerned he was just one more patient. However, the man in the bed opposite where he had been kept calling me over. I knew he had no need of me as he was ambulant and he was not on my list for medication, so

I kept putting him off, saying I would come round later. Eventually, about ten o'clock, the ward was settled down and I went over to him. 'You know that young man in the bed over there? He asked me to give you this and to ask you to phone him.' He handed me a slip of paper with a phone number on it which I pocketed and went through to the ward office. I had been left in charge of the ward and I began the business of writing up the report, but I kept looking at the phone number and wondering whether to dial it. I was between boyfriends at that time and although he seemed a very nice fellow, I knew nothing about him. Eventually I decided to call, thinking that I would decide what to say while the phone was ringing. Almost immediately, the phone was picked up and a male voice said, 'Hello.' Stammering somewhat, I said I was the nurse on the ward he had just left and was there something wrong. 'Oh no,' he said, 'I just wondered if you would like to come out with me.' 'Well, I am on night duty,' I said, 'so I suppose I could manage it.' And so we arranged to meet the next day.

He had a car and picked me up and we drove down to the coast. It was a lovely June day and as we strolled along the beach we exchanged information about each other. He was born and bred in Manchester, he said, and he had an older sister Margery, and a younger one called Miriam and a brother, six years younger than him called Tom. Margery was a Salvation Army officer and had recently married a man called Bram Jeavons. He himself was an engineer and had served in the British Army during the war in Italy during the Salerno landings and at Monte Casino. He had been part of the occupation forces in Austria and on his demobilisation he had considered going to work in Bahrein. At the last moment he had changed his mind and decided that he had a calling to be a Salvation Army officer. Thus I found out more about this organisation. His mother's family had been very active in the Army's early days in Manchester where

76

her parents had run a drapery shop. Her name was Martha Shepherd and she had married his father after he was invalided out of the First World War with an injury to the elbow joint of his left arm. He was a stonemason and had had his own business laying paving in the Manchester streets for some years.

Ronald had attended the Army's training college on Denmark Hill in London at a time when most of the trainees had been ex-servicemen and he had many tales of their devil-may-care irreverence. Each training session was given a name and his had been the King's Messengers. His first posting after being commissioned was to Cramlington, a mining village in Northumberland, where his enthusiasm had carried him through and had been very productive. His brand of humour came to the fore as he told me the tale of a funeral he had to conduct. 'It was pouring with rain,' he said, 'and as we stood there with the open grave rapidly filling with water, I turned to the man standing next to me and said, "I don't know whether to bury him or launch him," and to my horror, it transpired that it was the deceased's brother.' Such was the force of his personality that I am sure he managed to carry it off.

His next posting was to a small Corps only a mile or so from the large Newcastle Temple at the bottom of Westgate Road. It must have been felt by the powers that be that, following on his success in the mining community, he was just the man to blow a breath of fresh air into a bad situation. It seemed that there were two warring families in this church who would not speak to each other and who made the officer's life a misery. Perhaps such an experience was too much for someone recently released from Army service, but sufficient to say that he suffered a mental breakdown and resigned from the Salvation Army.

He was now working for the YMCA as an appeals organiser, hence the car which came with the job. He never said why he had not returned to Manchester – I could only guess – but he was very happy with his digs at the Toc H club where there were other like-minded young men with a view of the world bordering on that of disrespect.

Of course, not all of this came to light on our first outing. I enjoyed his company and we found that we both enjoyed singing and as the car toured the country lanes around Northumberland, his lovely tenor voice would blend in harmony with my soprano.

One of the lads at the Toc H was called Jimmy Froud, and occasionally I would take my friend Jean Clayton along on a foursome. She didn't have a steady boyfriend and Jimmy was good fun. On one occasion we went to a midnight showing of *For Whom the Bell Tolls* with Ingrid Bergman; at other times we would drive out to a pub, something I had not done since our Close House days.

Being on nights had its disadvantages and on more than one occasion when we went out, Ron would sit on the running board of the car smoking, while I curled up asleep on the back seat. Sometimes I would be able to get hold of a Dexadrine tablet from a friend working on the neurological ward. These had the effect of keeping me awake and fairly hyped up, it has to be said. In later years I expect they were what was referred to as 'uppers', although I never took 'downers'. Ron, however, always knew if I had taken one as my pupils would be very large, and he persuaded me not to do it any more.

Dorothy Waters was in a long-term stable relationship. Oddly enough, I knew all about her boyfriend, Frank. Frank was married to a girl called Mary who lived in the flat above Auntie Elsie in Biddlestone Road. Mary had been sent to America as an evacuee during the war while her elder sister, a great friend of Auntie May, had been in the Wrens. On her return, Mary probably found it hard to settle down in her parents' little flat in war-torn Newcastle, but it seems that one night she succumbed

78

to the blandishments of the local Lothario up against the backyard wall. When it was discovered that she was pregnant, it transpired that he was already married and Mary was left to carry the can. Enter Frank, who, feeling sorry for her, made an honest woman of her. This of course was at a time when being pregnant and unmarried was a fate worse than death. The marriage never stood a chance, they did not even live together, and now they were sitting out the long drawn-out experience of divorce. Meanwhile, Dorothy and Frank had to be most circumspect, as it wouldn't have taken much to upset the apple cart and have the divorce refused. Mary lived with her parents and her little boy and later married a bus driver, her Joe.

Doreen, ever the mystery, had no discernible social life, while Joan had a very nice boyfriend, a few years older than she was. Later she was to suffer from TB and had to give up nursing. Night duty was drawing to an end, but I had already made arrangements with my cousin Sheila to go youth hostelling for two weeks, heading for Devon and Cornwall. I was reluctant to go, but felt I could not let her down. The previous summer we had had a very enjoyable time hiking from hostel to hostel in the Borders, and we felt we wanted to see a bit more of the country. Hitch hiking at that time was an acceptable means of transport and the drivers of long distance lorries were always glad of a bit of company on their long boring routes in the days before motorways. On all the occasions that Sheila and I hitched rides, we never came across any trouble; all the men we met were great, often only too happy to talk about their families and produce their photos and to be as helpful as they could. So Ron drove us in the car through Newcastle and to the outskirts of Gateshead where he waited in a lay-by until a lorry stopped and picked us up. This one was going down to Yorkshire but he said he would be pulling in to a popular stop for drivers where he would ask around for a lift for us further south. The transport cafés were rough-and-ready places which served good hot food and before long we had changed over to a lorry going further south. Many drivers were happy to give a guided tour into the bargain and this one was no exception. As we passed around the outskirts of Birmingham he pointed out the area which he said was inhabited by all the wealthy people of the town. The houses were all in large grounds with impressive driveways, but soon we were headed further on and were passing Bristol Airport. There he showed us the Brabazon plane standing outside its hangar on the far side of the airport. It was huge and was obviously built before its time as it never went into service. We ended up in Wells, where he drove along the front of the cathedral where traffic could park in those days, and with many words of thanks, we left him and went to find the youth hostel. The next day we went to Cheddar Gorge and Wookey Hole, then made our way to Bath. We enjoyed that lovely city and tasted the waters from a glass at the fountain in the Pump Room, which at that time was a large unfurnished space. From there we descended to the baths themselves and dabbled our hands in the gently steaming water. I had harboured a wish to see Tintagel on the Devon coast, but as we made our way towards it, we were offered a lift which took us down to Cornwall instead and we spent a couple of nights in Polperro in a B&B, eventually coming back to Winchester, where we stayed in a youth hostel which had been an old mill. The washrooms were downstairs and outside along the mill race. Not a place to linger. Our road back took us through Oxford, where another kindly driver showed us the dreaming spires as we drove slowly through.

I arrived back to a passionate reunion and, while I did not realise it at the time, the last really carefree time of my youth.

On my return to work, I was told that I would be sent for a few weeks to a sanatorium in the countryside near

80

Stockton-on-Tees. Tuberculosis, the disease which had killed my mother, was still rife but inroads were being made on various forms of treatment. Apart from good food and plenty of fresh air, other treatments were being tried. The less invasive type was what was called an artificial pneumothorax, in which air was introduced into the space between the pleura and the lungs, so deflating the infected lung and, in theory, letting it rest and heal. More rigorous treatment was to operate and remove the infected lung. I was put on night duty and we had a higher ratio of nurses to patients, which made the work less onerous. One young man had a double whammy – he was also diabetic at a time when treatment was somewhat hit and miss and testing was not so sophisticated as it was later to become. He always had a bowl of powdered glucose and a teaspoon by his bed because if he went into a hypoglycaemic coma, it was known that he could be violent. In fact, on one occasion he had thrown himself through the ward window. So one night when I heard the yells of the other patients and found him throwing himself around, it took all my strength to hold him down and force some of the glucose into his mouth. Eventually I stabilised him, but next morning he said to me, 'Nurse, I wouldn't have struggled so much if you hadn't been holding me down.' Well, there was no answer to that.

Ron was able to come down and see me from time to time, and on one occasion we went to a beauty spot in Weardale where we picnicked and then roamed along the stream and up to the lovely waterfall. Crossing the stream at one point I stumbled and fell, knocking my head on the stones. As a black eye began to form, Ron took me back to the hospital where I went to find Matron to report my accident and to say I could not go on duty. This matron was universally disliked and was very strict and unfair with the nurses, so if I had expected any sympathy, I was to be disappointed. Instead she ordered me to go and change into my uniform and report for duty. I refused as I was suffering from a headache and blurred vision, and with Ron's help, went and packed up my things and he took me home. The next day I went to see Matron at the General and told her all that had happened. She asked me to make a written report, which I did. I was given a week off work and I heard no more about the matter. Whether the other matron heard about this or not, I never found out.

I was sent on to a surgical ward after that. There was a marked difference in the male and female wards ... apart, that is, from the obvious one! On a male ward, when the men were feeling better and were allowed to get up, they would take it on themselves to take the tea trolley round, dishing out the teas and collecting the dirty cups. This was a huge help as we were always so busy. On the women's ward, however, the ladies luxuriated in having their tea brought to them. Poor souls, I expect at home they were so busy caring for their families without so many of the conveniences that we now take for granted, that they made the most of someone looking after them for a change.

I was beginning to realise that Ron was going to be the one for me and he suggested that we should drive to Manchester and meet his parents. They lived in the suburb of Droylsdon and after a long drive, we pulled up in front of an end of terrace house with a small front garden off the main road called Edge Lane. Ron parked the car and together we walked up the path and he rang the door bell. A stoutish grey-haired lady opened the door, flung her arms around Ron and dragged him into the house, leaving me standing on the doorstep not quite knowing what to do. Eventually she deigned to notice me and I was given a rather grudging welcome. I had no way of knowing how long it was since he had seen his mother, nor really what his relationship with her was as he did not talk about her very much apart to tell me that she was 'all silver tea-set' but that wasn't my impression, as at the first opportunity she took care to tell me that she had a good name in the neighbourhood and had never owed anyone a penny. As I would have taken this for granted, I thought it rather strange. Eventually his father arrived home from work. Such a dear soul, with his broad Lancashire accent and his benign outlook on life, he was in complete contrast to his wife who seemed to be on her guard and distrustful of all and sundry. We stayed overnight and I was glad to leave the next day. On the way home I was having serious doubts about our relationship as, not having had the benefit of a mother, I had always looked forward to having a mother-in-law and to giving her all the love I had missed in my formative years and, hopefully, receiving back from her if not her love, at least her acceptance and the knowledge that I would not wish to take her son away from her but would be happy to be part of his family. However, it was obvious that that was not going to happen with this prickly woman who had no friends and who kept the rest of the world at arm's length.

Typically, Ron never got around to proposing to me in a formal manner, but in his usual humorous and irreverent way he asked me if I would be the mother of his children. It was not very long before it became apparent that that might very well be the situation in which I found myself. I had always been pretty regular in my menstrual cycle and when I missed a period and at the same time began to have very painful and swollen breasts, it didn't take an Einstein to work out what the problem was. Ron suggested I should go and see our family doctor, Dr Duncan on Heaton Park Road, and after examining me and questioning my dates, he said that it seemed quite probable that I was pregnant. Of course, this was in the days before the ubiquitous testing kit which gives the game away on every TV drama you can mention nowadays. So we decided that if my period hadn't arrived two weeks after it was due, then on Sunday, 29 October, we would speak to Dad and tell him we would be getting married as soon as possible. Of course as I was under the age of 21 his written permission was needed, but I had no doubt that he would give it and that he would give me all the support I needed.

On Tuesday, 24 October 1950, I was working until 9 p.m. and Ron came to pick me up at the hospital. We arrived back at Woodburn to find that neither Auntie Ethel nor my father were at home, but we hadn't been back for very long when there was a knock at the back door. I went to answer it to find two policeman standing there. They asked if they might come in and I brought them into the sitting room where Ron was sitting. 'Are you related to Mr William Trobe?' they asked. 'Yes,' I said, 'he is my father.' 'Is your mother here then?' they asked. 'No,' I said, 'she is dead. What is all this about?' 'I'm afraid there has been an accident,' they said. 'To my father?' 'Yes. Does he sometimes work on his lorries under the bridge?' 'Yes,' I said. 'Has there been an accident?'

The policeman seemed to draw himself up and he said, 'I'm afraid so.' 'And you think it is my father? Where has he been hurt? How bad is it?' I asked as my nursing instincts kicked in. 'It seems to be his chest. But we would like you to come with us to the hospital. We have a car outside.'

Quickly we got ready and left the house by the back door and walked to the gate leading to the main road. One of the policemen called to Ron and asked him to come and check that the back door was properly locked before we left and I walked up the steps and got into the back of the car as the policeman held open the door. Ron soon joined me and then as we moved off, he gently held me in his arms and told me that my father was dead. I don't remember any more of the journey to the Royal Victoria Infirmary, where we were taken to the mortuary. We were led along passages into a room with a bank of huge filing cabinets. One was pulled out and the sheet was lifted from the face and there I formally identified my dead father. I don't recall the journey home, but we got back to an irate Auntie Ethel wanting to know where everyone had been, as by then it was late at night. I had to break the news to her and in typical fashion, she kept a stiff upper lip and did not break down. I suppose she must have told the rest of the family but I don't remember when or how. I went to bed and the next day I phoned the hospital to tell them I would not be coming in. The rather slow assistant matron seemed to find difficulty in understanding my report that my father had had a fatal accident until I shouted down the phone, 'He is DEAD!' Ron took the phone from me and concluded the conversation. I later learned what had happened. My father was struggling to make a success of his business but often the trucks had to make deliveries of heavy loads onto uneven building sites, and despite the care they might take, the rear springs would be damaged. That night one of the drivers had returned his truck with a broken spring and as it was essential to my father to have the truck back on the road the next day, he tackled the repair in the dark and alone under the bridge where the trucks were parked. As he leaned over to replace the new spring, the jack which was holding up the body of the truck slipped and he was trapped. I believe that people coming out of the Playhouse across the road heard his cries and called for help, but it was too late. Auntie Ethel must have been in as bad a state as me, for after all, she relied on him for the upkeep of her home. Then there was the business and what to do about that and then … oh my God, there was May.

At last I told Ethel about her and about Doreen. Auntie Maryon was at the house by then and I knew that I would have to go to Alnwick and break the news to May. So Ron and I left and drove the miles to Alnwick with not a lot to say to each other. It was just so appalling and I had no idea how I was to tell May. Her father had died and they had left the pub by then and were living in a prefab building, just May, her mother and Doreen and of course were very surprised to see me. I asked May if I could speak to her alone and we went into her bedroom, followed by Doreen and as she sat on the bed I told her as gently as I could that my father had had an accident and that he had died the day before. She wailed with hysterical tears, Doreen began to cry too and her mother burst in to ask what was happening. I felt completely helpless in the face of such hysteria, but eventually, we calmed things down and May got ready and, leaving Doreen with her mother, she accompanied us to Newcastle. I brought her back to Woodburn where most of the family were gathered and she was introduced. Then we phoned the hospital and arranged for her to go to see my father. At the mortuary she flung herself upon his body in an agony of grief and had to be supported from the building. Uncle Harry had already taken over and was loud in his promise to pay for my father's funeral, a promise which did not materialise, but they asked my opinion on whether to have a burial or a cremation. With the memory of childhood visits to the cemetery to tend the graves of my grandparents and my mother, I opted for cremation.

During times of grief, memory plays many tricks, and I find it hard to put happenings in any sort of context. Obviously there had to be an inquest and this was not held until 16 November, and until then a funeral could not be arranged. However, a more pressing concern for Ron and me was my pregnancy and so, soon after having to absorb the fact of her brother's death, I had to tell Ethel of my pregnancy. Her immediate response was to wonder what her friends would say. Ron and I had not discussed how we would tell her, and on the spur of the moment I told her while we were alone. She held that against him and said that *he* should have told her, but by then I was beyond any such niceties. So as well as having to arrange my father's funeral, we now had to have her written permission, as my legal guardian, for our marriage. Armed with this we went to the registrar and then to the vicar of the church where my parents had been married and fixed a date for our wedding – 2 December.

What a conflict of emotions, grief for my father, happiness at my impending marriage, fear and some guilt about an unexpected pregnancy. I returned to work meanwhile and as I specialed a post-operative patient behind the concealing screens, I gave way to my grief and tears poured down my face. At work everyone was so kind. One of the porters, hearing that I was now an orphan, offered to have me come and live with himself and his wife. Dazed, I got through the days and to this day have no memory of my father's funeral. Afterwards, as the family congregated outside the crematorium complete with a distraught May, I asked Jean's parents, who had attended, if I could go with them to their house at Wylam as I could not face the gathering back at Woodburn. Although they must have been surprised, they did not attempt to dissuade me and so Ron and I left the crematorium and allowed the mourners to gather without my despair to stop them from talking over the whole affair.

After we received the death certificates, Auntie Ethel sent me up to the insurer's office on Heaton Road to deposit them and make a claim. As I was not yet 21 Uncle Harry as an executor was in charge and the business, meanwhile, continued to run.

My wedding was a very subdued affair. I went to town to choose a dress and a coat as it was winter. In deference to my loss, I chose a checked grey wool dress and a grey coat with a wine-coloured hat and I was to carry a small prayer book given to me by Jean's parents, dear souls that they were. Their kindness knew no ends and they were real Christians. Auntie Ethel ordered a small cake from the Co-op and the sandwiches were made at home. Jean and Dorothy were my bridesmaids, wearing their own clothes of course, and Uncle Harry took the photos and was to give me away. As we stood waiting for the car to come back and pick us up to go to the church, somehow the subject of Joyce's wedding came up and Uncle Harry waxed lyrical about the arrangements he had made for her. Finally he said, 'Now *that* was a wedding!' Obviously mine was a very poor thing in comparison. No doubt, had my father been alive, things may have been different, but how could you point this out to such an egotistical man? Ron had written and invited his parents but it seemed that his mother had taken exception to the way he had asked her. I never knew what he said and really, I couldn't have cared less if she chose to go into a huff. I had a lot more on my mind. I had continued to work out the men's wages, but as we were to go on a short honeymoon to a cottage on the Yorkshire moors, I showed Auntie Ethel how they should be done. However, when we got back she had just given the men a lump sum each and I had to sit down and calculate them all and do the adjusting.

Our honeymoon in the cottage started out with a heavy snowfall which covered the car, and so the next day we walked into the nearby village through a winter wonderland with glistening white snow and a brilliant blue sky. The cottage was very basic and we had much fun lighting a fire and trying to keep warm. Despite the dreadful start to our new life together, we were determined to overcome our difficulties and we faced the future with great optimism. At some point, I'm not sure when, Ron had ceased working for the YMCA so no longer had the car. He had also left the Toc H and was living at Woodburn as a lodger, so when we came back, Auntie Ethel was not willing to give us a room together and I used to squeeze in to his single bed. This could not go on, of course, so we found furnished rooms in an old flat in the west end of Newcastle. The flat was an upstairs one with an outside loo and no hot water system. The lady we rented from was a widow with one daughter who was married and lived near the hospital with her husband and daughter. We rather suspected that she, our landlady, had been an unmarried mother, as later in 1951 there was a census held and she and her friend had long deliberations about filling it in. She worked in a local grocery shop and we paid her £2 a week for two rooms and use of the kitchen. Ron had got a job as a production engineer at the Armstrong factory on Scotswood Road where he earned £5 a week. I spent a pound a week at the corner haberdashery shop where I had two dozen nappies put to one side with all the necessary sheets and nightgowns for the new baby. The other £2 was for our food and I would shop with some care down on Scotswood Road. I had, of course, left the hospital, but not without one final bit of spite from one of the assistant matrons. I had to go in to sign a form for some reason or other, and she left the room while I signed. When she came back she said she could not accept my signature because she had not witnessed it. So I brought the form away and took it to Uncle Harry's solicitor who was a member of the hospital board, and he witnessed it for me. I hope she got told off for that.

I attended the ante-natal clinic at the hospital and after the initial check up, it was to be some weeks before I had to go again. However, at that time, with TB being such a scourge in the country, mass-radiography units were set up. Anyone could go, but pregnant women were a priority, so I went to the appointment made for me. The X-rays were in miniature, but if something was found then you would be called back for a full chest X-ray. Somehow I wasn't surprised when I went down the stairs to pick up the post one morning and found a letter addressed to me. I sat on the bottom stair as I opened it, and sure enough, it was the call to go for a full chest X-ray. I kept the appointment and then it was a letter to go to my GP where I was told that I was suffering from TB. As it was in its early stages I was to be put on a regime of vitamin and calcium tablets and was to rest as much as possible. I was also to drink as much milk as possible and was given tokens with which to obtain extra milk. My mind went back to the young woman I had comforted the previous year when giving her her injections, and I wondered if that was where I had been infected. I religiously attended the clinic through the spring and early summer. The baby was due on 24 June, they said, then in the middle of June at the clinic, a different doctor with fingers like iron poked around at me then turned her head to me and said, 'Why haven't you been coming to the clinic?' 'I've never missed!' I spluttered, not understanding what was wrong, but it seemed that my baby was upside down and had already 'engaged'. There and then she sprinkled talcum powder on my abdomen and tried to forcibly turn my baby. I screamed and she had to stop, and with some impatience she said I would have to go for an X-ray and be brought in to have the turning done under an anaesthetic. It seems awful now, but then it was not realised how damaging X-rays could be, so off I was sent and my abdomen was X-rayed, showing that I was well and truly carrying a child in the breech position. A few days later I had to attend the clinic again and was taken down to the main theatre after the day's operations were finished. There I was given a general anaesthetic and when I came to, I found myself alone on the operating table. Feeling nauseous I heaved myself off, staggered over to the scrub-up basins, and with some satisfaction was sick in them.

I don't remember getting back home, but Ron was kindness itself. He put me to bed and went and made me a boiled egg, which, for his sake, I attempted to eat. Unfortunately, it all came back onto the tray. However, that was the least of my worries as it soon became evident that the backache I was experiencing was now creeping around to the front, with monotonous regularity. I got myself out of bed again and we sat in the living room timing my contractions, which seemed to be coming every five minutes. Ron went to our next-door neighbour as our landlady was out, and asked her to sit with me while he went out to phone for an ambulance. I felt a bit hysterical and I think the neighbour was just as bad, but soon Ron was back and before long the ambulance came. To my surprise the driver was Jack, one of our ex-employees, and he was most solicitous as he helped me in. Unknown to me, Auntie May and Auntie Elsie were just coming up the street to see how I was and were only in time to see me being carted off. It was late afternoon when I was admitted to a side ward, and apart from the occasional head around the door or a listen to my baby's heartbeat, I was left alone all night. Next day was the same. I had had nothing to eat for over 48 hours and I was famished so they gave me a saucer of powdered glucose and a teaspoon to keep my strength up. Eventually in mid-afternoon I was taken down to the theatre. A lady doctor examined me and said, 'What's it going to be?' 'A boy,' I said. 'That's what you think!' was her reply. I was wheeled into another theatre, the one I had been in the previous day, and the head gynaecologist arrived, all gowned and masked and accompanied by a bevy of students. I was asked if I minded, but at that point they could have had the King of Siam there and I wouldn't have cared. My legs were up on stirrups and in between the gas and air I was exhorted to push or sometimes not to as my daughter was born bottom first, and, with a great flurry of activity, her head was released with forceps. Then the afterbirth and then my episiotomy was stitched up. It was 10 minutes to 4 on 20 June 1951.

I was allowed a brief glimpse of my baby and then she was whisked away and I was cleaned up and taken up to the maternity ward on a trolley. I was put into a side ward on my own and fell into an exhausted sleep. At some point I was aware that someone had come in and talked to me

91

for a long time but I did not know what had been said. So when at last I woke up, a nurse came in with a large jug of water and another of milk and I was told to drink it all so that I could feed the baby. As I had previously been told that I probably wouldn't be allowed to I was delighted and drank the lot. Another nurse came in and I asked her who had come to talk to me and what had he said. She looked a bit alarmed and said she would call the doctor back. At last he came and sat down and explained to me that it had been decided that my baby would be given a vaccination against TB, this being a new drug that was being flown in specially from Sweden and that meanwhile, not only would I not be allowed to feed my baby, but I would also not be allowed to see her for six weeks when a test would be done to see that the immunisation had taken effect. With that he left me and when the evening visiting was allowed, Ron arrived to find me in floods of tears. The fluids I had drunk had swollen my breasts to mammoth proportions and I was in such agony that I had to have cold compresses on until such time as the hormone tablets I was given kicked in and dissipated the engorged milk.

It was at this point that I met the first of Ron's siblings. One afternoon, I was told I had a visitor and in walked Margery, Ron's eldest sister. Her husband's brothers and sister lived in Newcastle; in fact, Cyril and his wife Dorothy ran a successful musical shop in the town. Margery came, bringing me strawberries and her visit set the scene for any discussions with her in the future. There I was, stitched up, with breasts like footballs, deprived of my baby and suffering with TB but Margery couldn't wait to tell me what a terrible time she had had in giving birth to her son Bramwell the previous year. I had to sit and listen to a blow-by-blow description of every ache and pain, what the midwife said, how she had suffered, obviously no one had ever suffered such torments as she had. At last she went and in all the years that I have known her, there is not an ailment that you can mention but that Margery has not suffered far worse than you have.

Someone had to be found to care for my baby until I was allowed to have her and Auntie Elsie offered to take her. On the day she and Auntie May came to fetch her from the nursery, they came to see me at the door of my room and I had my second brief glimpse of my little girl. After they left I lay and sobbed on my bed and when Ron came in that evening he lay on the bed with me and held me while I cried.

In another couple of weeks I would be 21 and in the past year I had become an orphan, a wife and a mother. That carefree girl who had set off on her holiday to the south of England was gone and would never return.

7

Our daughter's name was to be Patricia Anne. We had laboured long and hard to choose a name – many were discarded because they invoked memories of disagreeable school contemporaries; family names were a non-starter – Ron's mother's name was Martha, mine had been Maud, my maternal grandmother had been Minnie and Grandma Wilson was Bridget. Ron was very keen to have a girl called after me, but I was reluctant for purely selfish reasons: I did not relish, in years to come, being referred to as 'Big Pat' as opposed to 'Little Pat', so a compromise was reached. She would have my name but she would be known by her middle name, Anne. Saints' names always appealed to me as being long-lasting and down to earth. So many names tended to date the recipient if the poor child was called after a famous person of the time. Of course, Princess Elizabeth had called her daughter Anne, but that wasn't why we chose it.

While I was still in hospital it was left to Ron to register our child and to my annoyance, he did so but came away with an abbreviated birth certificate. These certificates were really designed not to show the full parentage of the child and were a sop to children born out of wedlock so that it would not generally be known that they were 'bastards', the common term of the day. Illegitimacy was a terrible stigma for a child, but from Ron's point of view, as he told me, he had been very economical because they were cheaper. I had left him in charge of our modest finances and came home to find my simple but careful budgeting in chaos. No doubt, a lot of our income had gone on 'wetting the baby's head' at the local hostelry, but I could not praise him for saving money at the expense of our child's birth certificate. However, there was nothing to be done and I soon realised that keeping the financial ship afloat was going to be entirely up to me. He had obviously inherited a large dose of feckless Celtic genes, along with the charm and sense of humour which added to his attraction, while his dour mother's Lancashire caution had missed him by a mile. There was a woman who could make a penny do the work of ten.

With some economising I managed to bring our rent up to date once more so that we would have a roof over our heads and on the first weekend after my return home we set off by bus from the west end of Newcastle to my aunt's home on the far side of town. My breasts had settled down although I still felt as though my abdominal contents were likely to land on the floor at any moment, and so the long walk from the bus stop down the street to Auntie Elsie's flat was a slow one. Eventually we got there and at last I could have a closer look at my baby. She was beautiful. Perhaps because of the breech birth her little face was round and unmarked, and the care she was being given both by Auntie Elsie and Uncle Bob was unstinting. Afterwards, Ron and I had a quiet giggle at their enthusiastic description of her routine: 'She came up at 5 o'clock then after her bottle she went down at 6' – we had visions of a child made of rubber being bounced up and down during the course of the day. She was a very good baby, they said, and it was with some difficulty that we tore ourselves away. It was just too stressful to be so near and yet not to be able to hold her. There had been one drama; as the taxi had been bringing Anne and the aunts back from the hospital, Mary's little boy had jumped in front of it, causing the driver to brake suddenly and in those days before seat belts, Auntie Elsie in the back with Anne had had a hard job preventing her head from being smashed on the seat in front.

After my post natal-appointment, Ron had two weeks' holiday due to him and I asked Auntie Maryon if we could have the use of the cottage at Nenthead, to which she agreed.

We had used my father's car for our honeymoon, but were told it would have to be sold as part of his estate. I had used it for work for a little while and one of the sisters wanted to buy it for £100; however, I discovered that Uncle Harry had sold it to a friend of his for £60. As I was under age and he was an executor there was nothing I could do.

So we packed a small suitcase with sheets, pillowcases and a couple of towels as well as a modest change of clothing and caught the bus into town, making our way to the bus station near the railway station. There we caught the bus for Hexham where we had to change for the bus to Alston and Nenthead. The bus service was owned by the Wright brothers and they kept the access to the Allenheads valley and to Nenthead open to the small communities living there. The bus journey was beautiful that summer, with the breathtaking views at Staward Peel, and eventually we ground to a halt on the main road in Nenthead. The cottage was off the main road to the right and over the little stream coming down from the hills. There we walked along the small street; on the right the pub and on the left a row of terraced stone cottages. Our cottage backed on to the end of the row and had probably been the first one to be built facing across a little cobbled side street before the others were tagged on in a row behind it. Opposite was the large house where the local cobbler, old Mr Thompson, lived with his son Harris, Harris's wife Betty and their three children. Margaret was the eldest, about 12 years old at that time, then there was a son whose name I have forgotten and a younger son, Alan. Old Mr Thompson had made me a pair of clogs during the war with leather uppers and wooden soles satisfactorily studded with metal segs which made my progress heard far and wide. They were the most comfortable footwear I had ever owned. Now we entered the shop door at the side of the house where inside was dim and smelled of leather and beeswax and hardly had we greeted the old man before Betty erupted from the overstuffed living room behind. Betty could talk for England and was all agog to hear our news. I introduced her to Ron and eventually we left with the key and climbed the outside steps to the green-painted wood door to Dene Cottage. Inside the air was stale but dry and as I flung open windows and unpacked, Ron walked to the little grocery shop around the corner to buy milk and bread and whatever else was available. I stripped the bed, shook out the blankets and remade it with our sheets and pillowcases and when Ron came back we had a simple supper of bread and cheese That night we went to sleep wrapped in each other's arms with the windows open, lulled by the sound of the stream rushing past and the cries of the sheep up on the fells.

So for two weeks we left all our troubles behind and I wallowed in the peace and quiet and attempted to put all the sorrow behind me. We would take picnics up into the hills, paddle in the chilly stream and lie on the heather gazing up into the sky with its fluffy white clouds. Best of all was to have a home all to ourselves. Most couples had to start their marriages by living with their parents as they were put on the ever-lengthening council waiting lists, and although I had inherited the pair of flats, in the upper one of which I had been born, and Parkside, the house my father had built next door to Woodburn, they all had sitting tenants which the law of the land protected. On top of which, they all carried hefty mortgages which my father had used to try and get his business off the ground.

So as well as being a much-needed time in which to recharge our batteries, this was also a time to take stock of our lives and try to see where we were to go from here, for

97

certainly the life we had was not what we wanted for any longer than was necessary.

Nenthead is a small village set high in the hills; it is reputed to be the highest village in England and the road up the valley carried on over the top to drop down into Weardale and past old mine workings and the big wheel at Stanhope. The whole area had been a hive of industry in the 1700s and 1800s, when lead was mined under the auspices of the Quakers, who had built many of the houses for the workers. The side of the stream on which the cottage stood was known as Overwater and consisted of a curving street of cottages, a pub and a shop. On the other side of the stream and the main road was another pub, the Primitive Methodist Chapel and a long terrace of houses above the road where the post office was housed. Further down the main road towards Alston was the Co-operative Store with its large stock of pails, tin baths, brooms and rakes, as well as groceries. The lead mines had been dormant for many years but evidence of their existence could be seen up in the hills with the remains of old tramways, mysterious and gated tunnels into the hills and grass-covered mine dumps. However, in the centre of the village under a rather rickety corrugated iron roof there was a hive of activity where a company was busy extracting fluorspar from the mine dumps. Most evenings, Ron would walk across the street to spend an hour or so in the pub while I stayed at home with a book, for it was unthinkable for any woman to enter the pub. One night Ron came back in great excitement. He had, in his usual outgoing manner, been talking to the manager of the works and it transpired that in a month's time they would need a welder for the extraction plant. Ron was convinced he could do the job as well as anybody and meanwhile we could live at the cottage and have a proper home for the first time. We talked it over and decided that as soon as we had Anne back with us we would go for it.

The air was so pure, and although I had no discernible symptoms of my illness, no night sweats, no sputum, still the height at which the village lay, the good clean air and the fresh food had to be in our favour.

When we returned to Newcastle eventually the time came round for Anne to be taken to the hospital to be tested to see if her immunisation had taken. We were on tenterhooks, but all was well and we were given the all-clear for me to have my baby at last. However, Auntie Elsie wasn't so sure and she suggested to me that I should leave Anne there for a few more days and come down myself during the day so that she could show me what to do. Of course, there was no way I was going to agree to that; all my maternal instincts rose up at this challenge to the care of my child and in no uncertain terms I made it quite plain that Anne was to come to me at once. And so we hired a taxi and transported her and all her belongings to our rooms in the west end. What a joy to have her with us at last and finally to be a real family. Ron was as delighted as I was and would take a turn at bathing her in front of the fire. We had bought a second-hand bath made of papier-mâché, or some such material. This was before the days of plastic, and we had painted it ourselves, white inside and pink on the stand and the outside and it was easily transportable.

One evening after I had put Anne to bed, May and Elsie arrived at our flat. In later years I was sorry for the cruel way that I treated that dear soul who had stepped in and cared for my child so lovingly, but I wanted her all to myself and when Elsie asked if she could see her, I refused and said that she was already asleep for the night and I wouldn't disturb her. Possibly if she hadn't tried to persuade me not to take her away I might have felt more lenient, but I told myself that I was being cruel to be kind. I feel ashamed of what I did then; my only excuse that I was still so young and had suffered so much.

99

I celebrated, if that was the word, my 21st birthday on 15 July 1951, a very low key affair. Several birthday cards and small gifts from the family. Money was short for everybody at that time and I had already been the recipient of wedding gifts such as tea and dinner sets, some towels and a little cutlery, as well as gifts for the new baby, so I did not expect to receive anything much. However, now that I had reached my majority it was up to me to start sorting out my father's estate. The business had been wound up in March but probate had still not been granted. Of the properties I had been left, Parkside had been valued at £1,000 and the pair of flats at Warwick Street at £600. However, both carried hefty mortgages, raised in order to start the business; in fact, the one on the Warwick Street property was for almost £593. I took up collecting the rents again. The downstairs flat was let to a single lady who lived there with her mother. She worked at the local library, a huge Gothic building just a short walk away, and she also collected the rent from the upstairs tenant. On my first visit to her, she said I should come and have a look at the kitchen where, indeed, the damp was running down the walls. She was concerned as her mother was elderly and not too well. I told her there was little I could do, but when I got back home I gave it some thought. The money from both the rents only just went to pay the mortgage, and we had no spare money to pay for repairs. I therefore decided to put a proposition to her, and after discussing it with Ron, the next time I went to collect the rents I suggested that she might be interested in taking on the property herself, if it could be arranged that she would take over the mortgage and pay the legal costs. She was somewhat taken back, but I explained that there was no way I could afford any repairs, so she promised to give it some thought. Eventually, the next time I called she said she would agree to the arrangement, and so it was done.

That was one worry off my mind, but Parkside was also

a problem. Auntie Nancy, my Uncle Stan's widow who had remarried and was now living in Newlands, the house next door, had been badgering me for a share in expenses to some flashing on the roof, but before I took over this was discovered to be a matter for the house insurance and the work was undertaken without my being involved. The mortgage on this property was just under £750. The main problem was getting the rent out of the tenant, a distant relation of Sheila's father. Often it needed a solicitor's letter costing a guinea before the arrears would be settled. But there was nothing to be done about that at the time.

Probate was finally settled at the end of July, just before we were to have Anne back. May had made a claim on the estate on Doreen's behalf. I was happy about this as when my father had told me about May all those years ago, he had also told me that he had given May a letter stating that she should have 10 shillings a week for Doreen until she was 16, so I felt that the £300 she received was fair and just. While £300 may not sound like very much by today's standards, in 1951 it would have gone a long way towards buying a modest property in a rural area like Alnwick. Had my father wished to change his will in any other way, he could have done so, but after all, I was the one who had helped him with his business, typed his letters and done the accounts when I would much rather have been out with my friends. However, I think May, having a very inflated opinion of my father's financial worth, thought that I had come away with the lion's share of the spoil, not knowing the many problems I was left to deal with.

At last we were able to make our move to Nenthead and settle down in the cottage, but before we went Ron had been scouring the national newspapers for a job and he had sent off an application to the Division of Atomic Energy who were looking for progress engineers to help in the building of atomic energy factories in various parts of the country.

Although the cottage was very basic – we had no bathroom and managed with a good wash down, spreading a towel on the floor of the living room – I coped with a baby quite well. In the morning I would boil water on the open fire and prepare her bath. After she was fed and settled outside in her pram, I would add more water to the bath and wash her nappies and clothes and hang them out on the line near the stream. Our linen and Ron's shirts went on the bus to Alston where there was a laundry which was very reasonable. We decided to have Anne christened at the little Primitive Methodist Church in the village, where the minister came from time to time to conduct the services. It was a lovely day when we walked with her to the church. She wore a beautiful little dress that Auntie Nancy, Harry's wife, had bought for her and we had bought a christening cake at the Co-op. We invited everyone we knew to tea afterwards and it was a splendid occasion.

I was in my seventh heaven, with a home to ourselves, a loving husband and an adorable baby. Only one fact cast a shadow. I knew how sneaky tuberculosis could be and that it could, without any warning, suddenly decide to take wings and devour the lungs. I had suffered by being an only child, always feeling I was the one left out and envying my friends their close family ties. And so I persuaded Ron that we should try for another baby straight away. I reasoned that once more, a pregnancy would become another pneumothorax, thus resting my lungs, and besides, it might take several months to conceive. In the event, we hit the jackpot first time around, and before Christmas came, I knew I was pregnant again.

My friends Dorothy and Jean were in the throes of taking their final exams; Stella, after she left school, had gone on to university and now had a BA. She had married Jack Alder, a lecturer at one of the local colleges, and they had bought a brand new house on an estate being built in the west end of Newcastle. She had had a miscarriage in the first year of their marriage. They came to visit us at the cottage, and Ron and Jack went across to the pub where, on the wall, was a calendar with a photo of the Matterhorn. Jack kept everyone enthralled as he told them of being in a group who had made the climb.

After she had passed her finals, Dorothy was finally able to marry Frank and they had to live with Frank's parents in their small flat, where they had a bed settee in the front room. Dorothy later became theatre sister at the General and Jean became ward sister on the children's ward at Walkergate Hospital. We had all moved on, and soon events were about to speed up even more.

One morning, a letter came in the post asking Ron to go to Risley in Cheshire for an interview. I waved him off and a few days later he returned. The interview had gone well and he thought he might be in line to be selected. Just before Christmas, the news came: he was to start at the headquarters at Risley in the New Year. There were single quarters available for him as an interim measure, so I moved back to Newcastle again with Anne. Auntie Elsie, of course, was delighted to see me and I hope she forgave me and understood my treatment of her before. My father's estate was now wound up and we had some money available. Ron had a habit of cashing cheques as though all the resources of the bank were his to command, so he had a bit of an overdraft. We were able to get some money to pay it off and to cover the costs of our next move. The first thing was to find a house, so I went down to Manchester with Anne and we stayed with my mother-in-law while we went house hunting. Warrington was some distance from Manchester so it took some time to get there by bus and train. On the first day, Mother-in-law offered to look after Anne while we went to find an estate agent. Nothing we saw was up to much so we planned to go back the next day. However, she said she couldn't look after Anne again, so we had to take her with us. No easy task as she had to be carried everywhere on buses and trains and out to view property and on top of that I was pregnant. So it had to be now or never and we chose a house which in other circumstances would not have been our first choice; number 2, Jackson Avenue was a typical semi in the suburbs with not a great deal to recommend it.

I returned to Newcastle for a while until the legal niceties were completed. The furniture from my parents' house had been spread around at the time the house was emptied prior to it being let at the outbreak of the war. Some had gone to furnish Auntie Maryon's bungalow at Sparty Lea and it was just not going to be viable to recover any of that. Some, however, was at Woodburn and I let Auntie Ethel know that I would be wanting it. Primed by May and Elsie, who knew *exactly* what had been my mother's, I laid claim to a bedroom suite and to a pretty little desk with drop-down flap and a china cabinet above. When later the time came for us to move in, we hired a furniture van to collect these items as well as some of the bits and pieces we had bought when we were first married and which were at Auntie Elsie's. Meanwhile, to be nearer to Ron in his bachelor quarters, I moved down to Manchester to stay with his parents. I did my best to be as friendly as possible with my mother-in-law and we got on reasonably well. However, I couldn't help noticing how she criticised her family to me; being young and naïve, it was some time before it dawned on me that in my absence, she probably had just as many criticisms of me. Her favourite tirade against Ron, given with a great shake of the jowls, was, 'I never had a penny out of him'. Apparently when he lived at home after leaving the army, he would give her money for his board but borrow it back from her before the week was out. That sounded like Ron!

Younger sister Miriam was staying with friends. It seemed that she and her mother had had words because Martha didn't like the young man she was courting. Ronnie was a close friend of Ron's and was as big a tearaway. Both, along with younger brother Tom, were at one time members of the Salvation Army band at the Manchester Citadel. Ronnie had been a paratrooper but was invalided out with stomach ulcers. He had trained as a painter and decorator but was unable to follow that profession as the paint fumes upset his stomach. He was in the process of trying out a new career as a stationery salesman. Tom was living and working in Cheltenham and was courting a young lady called Iris. Margery and Bram were Salvation Army officers at Walsall but were having a lot of trouble with their young son Bramwell who was still a toddler. It seemed that he suffered from terrible eczema and on one occasion when they had been visiting Martha, when fresh fish was brought into the house his whole body erupted with painful sores. At night Margery had to smear ointment on his arms and legs then put cardboard splints on his joints and tie him to the cot sides to prevent him scratching himself raw.

Before he had been born, my parents-in-law had gone on holiday with them to Jersey by plane. This was quite something in those days and it seemed that Bram had the wherewithal to do it. Many years later Margery told me that Bram had wanted to buy a property in Jersey and asked Martha to go in to it with him. While at first agreeing, she later changed her mind, much to Margery's dismay. It would have been a good little earner. Apparently during the war, refugees from Jersey had come to Manchester during the German occupation and links had been made and kept up once they returned home after the war. Now there was some talk that Margery and Bram, would be sent to South Africa by the Army, Bram to take over the running of the Appeals section from the headquarters in Johannesburg.

Eventually moving day came and we finally took possession of our own home. We had taken out a small mortgage as

105

the bulk of the purchase price came from what my father had left me. The neighbours adjoining our house were an older couple of whom we didn't see a great deal. The house on the other side of us was owned by a couple about our age – at least the husband was about Ron's age, the wife a bit older than me. We got on very well and I think she was glad of a friend as many of the locals were wary of her. She was German and she had met her husband when he was in the occupation forces after the war. They had two little boys, one about four and the other a little bit older, but both were the image of their father with jet black thick straight hair and identical features. She would often invite me in for a coffee in the morning as her husband was an agricultural salesman and was usually away all week. By ten in the morning her house would be spick and span, the washing out on the line and not a hair out of place – unlike me. I always seemed to be on the point of, but not quite, catching up with my chores, no matter how hard I worked. Often she would keep an eye on Anne, with her pram wheeled into her garden if I needed to catch the bus into town to pay bills or run some errand.

I attended the local clinic every week, which was quite a long walk but essential as it was here that I could buy the cheap powdered milk for Anne as well as the bottles of cod liver oil and concentrated orange juice. The government was determined that children should grow up with strong, healthy bones and to wipe out the scourge of rickets which had been the curse of some areas in the 1930s. Mothers were encouraged to put weight on their babies and Anne did well, putting on a pound or two at every visit. I had also signed up with the local midwife as I was to have my next baby at home. We got on very well, but I was a bit disconcerted when it turned out that in all probability she would be on holiday when my baby would be due. Sure enough I went into labour before she was back and as we didn't have a telephone at that time

Ron went off to phone the midwife. I should explain here that our house was number 2, Jackson Avenue, but was situated at the apex of two roads, the one on the left having another name, which I don't recall. The new midwife, not knowing the area, went to number 2 of the street on the left, and not getting any answer to her knock, and finding the back door open, she went upstairs where she began to unpack her bag beside the person huddled in the bed. Suddenly, the body woke and sat up with a start and she found herself face to face with an unsuspecting night worker complete with five o'clock shadow. So when she arrived at our house and she told us the tale we were all in hysterics! Ron had also phoned his mother who had promised to come down and help, much to my surprise, and she arrived just as I began to go into the final stage of labour. The midwife called to Ron and he came upstairs and encouraged me during the final lap. I gave one almighty push and the baby shot out and slid down the bed as though water skiing on the collection of amniotic fluid on the rubber sheet. 'It's a boy,' the midwife shouted and at 7lbs 8oz Paul arrived about midday on a Monday morning. Mother-in-law came dashing upstairs but couldn't hide her disgust that Ron had been present at the birth. This was not the done thing in those days and I seem to remember that it even got a small piece in the local paper on the subject. Ron was given the job of burying the afterbirth in the garden, while Mother-in-law took the soiled sheets and put them through the washing machine. Once they were hung out, she gathered up her handbag and went back home, so the day after my son was born, I sat on the edge of the bed and did the ironing.

I was not allowed to feed Paul either, although it seemed that my TB had healed itself. Paul did not respond well to the bottle and was a very colicky baby, giving us many disturbed nights. Once, desperate for sleep, I wrapped him warmly in his blankets, tucked him into his pram and wheeled it through the kitchen and into the wash-house at the back. I then closed the wash-house door, the back door, the kitchen door and our bedroom door before going to bed and getting a good night's sleep. It didn't seem to do him any harm.

We had a lot of visitors to our house. Auntie May and Auntie Elsie came for a week and Ron's brother Tom and his new wife Iris came from Cheltenham, where they had a caravan in a farm yard. Iris's father was a farm labourer and she came from a large family of one brother and several sisters. It was the first time we had met and she told me that Mother-in-law had come to their wedding but had cried loudly all the way through. I was quite pleased then that she didn't come to mine as while the bride's mother is allowed to shed a discreet tear or two, it isn't very complimentary to the bride for the bridegroom's mother to make a fuss! Ron's sister and her husband Ronnie, also newly married, came occasionally, but Miriam was a bit of a reflection of her mother and could be very hypercritical if things did not come up to her high standards.

All in all, I was very happy as I had a husband I adored and who loved me, I had a daughter and a son and we had our own home, no mean achievement in those days of austerity. We even had an old second-hand van painted bright blue with a red door and the summer after Paul's birth we would load his pram into the back of the van as the handle folded down and we would drive to Hoy Lake where the children enjoyed splashing around in the shallows as the tide crept in over the miles of sand.

I found caring for the children and all the housework very tiring. We had a tiny washing machine which only washed the clothes. They then had to go through the wringer and be rinsed in a tub of water and rinsed again before being hung out to dry in the garden. One day I took the second load out to hang up only to find that the clothes line had snapped and all the nappies and sheets had fallen into the muddy flower beds. I sat down and cried. I couldn't understand why I felt so tired until one morning as I stood at the sink washing up the breakfast dishes, I looked at my face in the tiny mirror on the window sill and there staring back at me was a washed-out face with great circles under the eyes. I realised something was wrong so made an appointment with the doctor. After another chest X-ray it transpired that I had a flare up of the TB. This time I was to have three months' bed rest and a course of PAS and daily streptomycin injections.

This caused some problems as we had no relatives nearby and our income was not so large that we could afford full-time help. The solution was to let our two front rooms as furnished accommodation and employ someone to come in and clean and look after the children. We put an advert in the local paper and an American couple came to share our home. The husband was employed at the nearby airforce base and his wife and baby son had come out to be with him. They were a lovely couple, the wife from one of the southern states, which was reflected in her laid-back effort to any sort of organisation. Her poor child was forever falling off their bed where she had dumped him while she made up her face. They had the two front rooms and often the curtains remained closed all day. As this was an indication that someone had died, poor Ron was an object of some sympathy, so that I had to ask her, if she did nothing else, would she please open the curtains! Everyday things were in very short supply for us, while she could shop at the PX on the base as well as take advantage of the enormous resources available in the gigantic Sears Roebuck catalogue. They stayed with us beyond the time that I was up and about again and one day I came in to the kitchen to find an almost-full dish of stuffed eggs dumped in the kitchen sink. I surreptitiously rescued as much as I could!

Ron's job was as a progress engineer for the Division of Atomic Energy. At that time several plants were being built with a view to providing energy for the country for many years to come. Ron, along with many more young men, went around the country visiting the factories that were making the components for the plants, to check on their progress and to chivvy them along. On occasions when there were strikes at the factories, he had to take the work from them and have it done elsewhere as they were working to a very tight schedule. There was also a heightened sense of security in view of several well-published outings of Russian spies and the infiltration and passing on of state secrets. Ron liked to tell the story of one of his compatriots who, travelling by train to his destination, left his briefcase behind. This caused a bit of an incident as the front was emblazoned with the departmental logo and when it was retrieved and he went to collect it, he was asked to unlock it and check the contents in front of several security-conscious police. Reluctantly he opened it and withdrew a pair of pyjamas and his toilet bag. Whether this was true or not I cannot tell, but with his Irish lineage, Ron would never let the truth get in the way of a good story.

Paul was taking longer than Anne had done to walk, largely I think because he could crawl so well, not actually on his hands and knees, but on hands and feet. Our American lodgers sometimes brought friends, another couple, over to visit and we would have a bit of a party, now that I was up and about again. One night, Paul had woken up and been brought downstairs where he happily crawled around as we laughed and joked. The Americans had brought a bottle of Canadian V.O. whisky with them and Paul, unseen by us, had found a glass on the floor by the side of one of the chairs and had helped himself. The next thing we knew, he came out from behind the chair, walking for the first time. It seemed all he had needed was a bit of Dutch courage.

Eventually our lodgers were replaced by an English couple. The husband was in the Navy, his wife came from Cornwall and we all got on very well. She taught me how to make Cornish pasties. After Paul's birth we became eligible for Family Allowance, 8 shillings per week, which I would pick up at the post office and deposit at the little haberdashery next door which sold children's clothes. When I had enough saved up I would buy them look-alike outfits and they were much admired as I took them round the shops in their pram. Shopping had to be done every day as we had no fridge, and household freezers were not to come for many more years. Although many things were in short supply, a local bakery had set up shop and their cakes were in great demand. Shopping there always meant a long wait in the queue. One day I left Paul in the pram outside the shop, something everyone did in those days, and took Anne in with me while I waited in the queue. To my horror when I came out, both Paul and his pram were gone! I rushed back into the shop to ask if anyone had seen anything. No one had. The shopkeeper phoned the police while kindly women comforted me. The police came in a car and drove me up and down the streets to see if we could see anyone. Finally they suggested we should return to our house as Anne by this time was fretful. We arrived there to see Paul's pram parked outside. I rushed in and there he was, being looked after by my lodger. Apparently she had come past the shop while doing her own shopping, seen Paul, and decided to wheel him home *along with her own son in his pram* and no one had noticed! Needless to say she got the rough edge of my tongue as well as a telling off by the police, but what a relief to find Paul safe and well.

We hired a car on one occasion, and drove to Newcastle to visit the family and to show off the children. I was able to take a snap of Grandma Wilson with her first great-grandchildren. On another occasion we went down to Cheltenham and stayed with Tom and Iris in their caravan.

At home, Paul and Anne shared the small bedroom, the

box room, as the estate agents would call it, over the front door. They had a cot each, placed so that when they awoke they could look out of the window at the men passing on their way to work and would have great fun waving to them all. Paul managed to make a small hole in the curtain on his side and I went in one morning to find him with his head through the hole and the curtain twisted so that he was in danger of strangulation. On another occasion I went in to find him clinging to the side of his cot as he had undone all the screws and the bottom had all but fallen out.

In 1953, we bought one of the first television sets in our area, a 9-inch screen Bush, which involved much shouting and running up and down stairs as Ron adjusted the aerial to get a clear picture. We would sit glued to its little black-and-white square and dash to the kitchen to put the kettle on or go to the loo every time the programme paused and the interlude came on. I was fondest of the one showing a stream and rippling waterside plants, although the seashore came a close second. We crammed the living room full of friends and neighbours as we watched the coronation of our youthful Queen.

Things were moving on for Margery and Bram. The Salvation Army had indeed sent them to South Africa and they were living in Johannesburg. We heard glowing reports of their life there and of the availability of fresh fruit and tinned goods that we could only dream of. Some time after they had gone, the in-laws, to everyone's astonishment, decided to go too. As they rented their house it did not take them long to sell up. At that time there were no facilities to take all one's furniture; a couple a tea chests and a cabin trunk were the extent of one's luggage. They came to stay with us for the last week or so before they left and they offered to have the children for a day so that Ron and I could have a trip away. We had no car at that time, so we booked a bus trip to Blackpool. Unfortunately it wasn't a very nice day and we had very little money, so spent most of the day huddled in one of the shelters on the promenade out of the rain. In addition, we seemed to have very little to say to each other as our lives were so separate. We went to the station at Manchester to see his parents off, poor Martha wailing all the way. As they settled in, letters began to arrive telling of the good life to be had there. Emigration was on the minds of many young people at that time; there was unease over Russia and its threat to the West, the Cold War and the Iron Curtain loomed in our thoughts and I had no wish to be parted from my children if evacuation became necessary again. We were aware that we could all be obliterated in an instant should an atomic bomb be dropped and it was common knowledge that there were safe places for the government and the Royal Family to be taken to in the event of a nuclear war. Many took the option to go to Australia on the £10 passage, but that seemed too far away to me, as did New Zealand. Canada seemed to exchange a colder climate than the one we knew, while Northern Rhodesia seemed a likelihood as Ron could easily get a job there in the mines.

One morning before Ron left for work, a letter came from his parents. We opened it up sitting together at the foot of the stairs. Martha wrote that they had been talking to their doctor, who it seemed, was a son of General Smuts, and they had told him of my health problems. He told them that if I could get to South Africa I need never worry about a relapse of TB again. We read the letter through twice. I looked at Ron, he looked at me, and we said as one, 'OK, let's do it!'

8

It was never going to be easy or straightforward to arrange to emigrate to South Africa. We wrote to the folks already there, but of course their transition had been somewhat more simple than ours would be. Bram and Marge, as Salvation Army officers, did not own either their home or their furniture and the official practicalities were taken care of by the Salvation Army. Mam and Dad had only needed to sell their furniture and give up the lease on their rented house. We had a house to sell, Ron would have to have a job to go to, and my health problems would have to be taken into account. We began by contacting South Africa House to apply for residence, and as we wanted to be straightforward from the start we told them of my treatment for TB. They requested X-rays and a doctor's report before we could be considered and we waited anxiously for the reply. I would be admitted as a temporary resident on a renewable six-monthly residence and on deposit of a sum of £50. Ron would have to provide proof that there was a job waiting for him on arrival.

This hurdle having been passed, Bram, who was appeals organiser for the Army in South Africa and as such made contact with many business firms in Johannesburg, undertook to provide a job offer in one of the factories. On its receipt we put our house on the market and suffered a nail-biting time until we found a buyer. As house prices were very static in those days, there was no money to be made on the sale; instead, it was an expensive business as the estate agent's and solicitor's fees had to come out of the sale price.

114

The house in Newcastle was still a problem as the rents barely covered the mortgage repayments or any necessary repairs. However, Auntie Maryon offered to buy it from me for what was left on the mortgage as well as paying the legal costs herself, so that was one less thing to worry about. Our permits had arrived and we went into Manchester to visit the Union Castle offices to book passage. At the same time we had to sell our furniture; there wasn't much, but I was saddened to part with my mother's little desk with its pretty china cabinet above. The lady who ran the haberdashery where I used to buy the children's clothes finally bought that at a knock-down price. One amusing incident happened at that time. Most goods were still in short supply and I wanted a cabin trunk to hold the bulk of our personal possessions. Someone told me that there was a lady living on the main road whose daughter had just come back from South Africa and it was felt she may have one to sell. I knocked at the door and the young lady in question came to speak to me. I told her what I was after and she was most interested to know that we were going to South Africa having just come back from there. 'Oh, Jo-burg,' she said in a broad Lancashire accent. 'They call it Jew-burg, you know. You won't laike it, I say, you won't laike it.' A bit taken aback, I said, 'Well, would you be prepared to sell me your cabin trunk then?' 'Oh no,' came the reply, 'we're going back next month!'

Finally the furniture was sold, our cases packed and Anne, to my amusement, would stuff her dolls into any case she found open. We were to stay with Miriam and Ronnie in Manchester until our departure and we took the opportunity to go to Newcastle for a last Christmas as we were to sail in early January 1954. Miriam had not had any children at that time and was very house proud. Ronnie had decorated their house with lovely wallpaper and she carefully covered all the lower walls with lining paper in case any sticky fingers came near. Ron was working his notice and Miriam

115

and Ronnie were both at work. One day, having cleaned up in the kitchen, I couldn't see the children but followed the sound of giggles which were coming from behind the closed toilet door at the head of the stairs. Trying the door I found it to be locked and, horror of horrors, there was the sound of splashing water. Trying to keep as calm as I could, I called to them through the door and, having got their attention, as persuasively as possible said, 'Pull the little lock along, darling' (it was a bolt). More giggles and water splashing, then, 'Come on sweetheart, pull the little lock along,' all the time desperately wondering if I could get access through the tiny loo window, always supposing I could find a ladder. Finally, to my relief, little fingers fumbled with the lock, the door opened and I was able to mop up the floor before Miriam came home to inspect for any damage. On another occasion, as I got them ready to walk to the shops, I dashed back into the house for my bag. When I came back out there was no sign of Paul. He must have been able to crawl underneath the gate as he was eighteen months old at the time. I ran out into the street, fortunately a quiet one, but there was no sign of him. I dashed to the left and, out of the corner of my eye down a little pathway between the houses spotted an energetic little figure rapidly disappearing around a corner. Another moment and I wouldn't have been able to see where he had gone.

We were to leave Manchester for London by train the evening before we were due to sail. It was a sleeper, which seems strange now, but in the early 1950s journeys were not always straightforward. The train was put into a siding in London and we were able to sleep until morning then make our way to the boat-train terminal. There had been a very hard frost and the train to Southampton was desperately slow. Eventually we pulled into the docks, where all was confusion. Our luggage had gone on ahead of us and we checked in at the dockside with all our paperwork. My passport from

116

that time makes me look very glamorous rather than the 23-year-old harassed mother that I was. We had been telling Anne that we were to go on a big ship and so we walked up the covered gangway and into the spacious reception area from where we were directed to our cabins deep down in the ship. A seaman came along to see us settled in and gave us a pep talk about seasickness which, according to him, was all in the mind. I was to remember that as all four of us sat on the floor of our cabin taking turns with the bucket as we lurched through the Bay of Biscay. Once we were settled in we went up on deck to watch the boat leave our homeland and to take a last look at England. We were told that because of the hard frost, many people had missed the boat because the points on the railway had been frozen, so we were doubly glad that after all the hassle we had made it. We watched as the anchor was pulled up and the hawsers attaching us to the docks were released. The tug boats were in place and gradually began to pull the ship away from the docks. As the space grew wider, Anne began to cry bitterly and wouldn't be pacified. I lifted her up to comfort her and she pointed at the tugs and demanded to go on the boat. She had not realised that we were actually on one, it was so big and more like a hotel. We stood in the bitter cold and watched the shoreline gradually disappear. Did I have a lump in my throat? I really don't recall. Probably not, because without mother, father, brother or sister to leave behind, I had with me all the people I cared about, and we had set out on a great adventure.

Much of life on board centred around mealtimes. Parents took their children to a separate dining room and supervised them, after which they were taken to the nursery where staff looked after them while the parents went to have their meal in the main dining room. Anne was delighted with all the toys and playthings supplied, but 18-month-old Paul resented being dumped and made no secret of the fact. His roars followed us down the stairs as we went to find where we would be seated. The dining room stretched across the full width of the ship, with large windows along each side. Each place was provided with a printed menu and we were treated to food the like of which we had seldom seen during those days of austerity. Fresh fruit was provided in our cabins and mid morning we were encouraged to go up on deck and be tucked up on enormous wooden deck chairs and served with hot Bovril. I will draw a veil over the passage through the Bay of Biscay, except to say that in the dining room, strips of wood were unfolded from under the sides of the tables to prevent everything sliding off onto the floor and as we wallowed through the rough seas, first one wall of windows would dip below the surface then rise, while the other side plunged down in a haze of green. After we had recovered from our bout of sickness, our appetites returned and we were able to eat again, but the dining room was very sparsely populated for several days.

Fortunately we had brought reins for Paul as he determinedly dashed in all directions. The ship's rails, and later the swimming pool, were vastly attractive and without the reins I doubt he would have survived the journey. It was a sight to behold when he made his busy way along the corridors near our cabin; as the ship swayed he adjusted his gait to right or to left like the most experienced of sailors. As the first day or two passed, we gradually left behind the lowering skies, patches of blue appeared, the temperature rose and the clouds changed to fluffy white billows above us.

In the evenings, I could put the children to bed after they had had their evening meal and their bath and stewardesses would patrol the corridors and come and tell me if one of them was crying. This was marvellous and we were able to socialise and meet up with some of our fellow passengers. We sat at a table in the lounge with a couple whose accent I recognised immediately as belonging to fellow 'Geordies'.

118

Val and Cynthia Brennan were travelling to Cape Town where Val's insurance company was sending him to work. They came from the west end of Newcastle so we had never met before but we got on famously. Soon the ship docked at Las Palmas and we were able to enjoy our first trip ashore. We collected the children and, suitably dressed in lighter clothes than we would normally have worn, we walked around the town. The main place of interest was the church, where visitors were encouraged to go up the tower in a lift. Out of interest, as we ascended, Val read the notice pasted on the inside which informed us that the lift was last checked in 1935. Fortunately for us it got us to the top without any problems and we were able to look across the harbour and see our floating home being refuelled where, we had been told, it was cheaper than in the UK. After the visit to the church we took a taxi up into the hills to walk around and let the children roam. There was very little to see, just a bit of scrubland, but of course, in years to come it would all blossom as a tourist attraction.

We set sail from Las Palmas, myself complete with a large straw hat I had bought there, resuming our journey to our new future. There was a fancy-dress competition where the children were also to compete. I hadn't much idea what to dress them up as, but Cynthia was a mine of information. We purchased rolls of crêpe paper from the shop and Cynthia made Anne a costume of a little Dutch girl, with blue skirt, white apron and a Dutch hat. I wanted to make Paul the baby in the Fairy soap advertisement, but needless to say the shop did not sell bars of Fairy soap so he had to make do with just wearing his nappy. Anne won first prize, however, and claimed her kiss from the captain. A young French girl who was travelling alone arrived at the evening dinner dance wearing a beautiful crêpe dress, as Marie Antoinette, and was given a round of applause.

A few days later we watched the celebrations as we 'crossed

119

the Line' and Father Neptune threw as many people as possible into the swimming pool after they had been smothered in shaving foam and 'shaved' by his black assistant.

Our sister ship passed us on its return journey to the UK and we all stood and waved and cheered it as it passed.

Much of my time was taken up in the bowels of the ship doing the washing and the ironing. Both the children were potty trained but Paul needed some night-time protection so there were always clothes to be seen to. But by and large, it was a wonderful interlude with splendid meals such as we had not seen for many years and day after day of wonderful sunshine spent lazing beside the pool and entertaining the children.

The day we were due to arrive in Cape Town we were up early to watch our landfall. Dawn was just about to break as we approached the land and there before us was the majestic outline of Table Mountain and below it, the flickering lights of the town. As we drew closer the light grew stronger and we could make out the shapes of the pastel-coloured houses strewn up the slopes of the hill. As we were not disembarking there, we were able to continue to watch as the ship slowly edged her way to the quayside and finally tied up in an area which was sparse and lacking any buildings. The waterfront was on reclaimed land and it would be some years before buildings sprang up. At that time the end of the main street, Adderly Street, could be seen from the quayside. We were to be there for two nights and we had arranged to meet Cynthia and Val the next day. We had obtained a map of Cape Town on the ship, and with all the confidence in the world, chose a beach on which we would meet. Cynthia and Val were to be met at Cape Town, where Val was to work for his insurance company, while we were to sail up the coast to Durban. Later that day we went into Cape Town and wandered around the shops, calling into a café for a cold drink where Anne drew many stares for her blonde hair and pale skin. The next day, we took a taxi, and sure enough, met up with our friends and spent a pleasant day with a picnic supplied by the ship. We were shocked, however, at how cold the sea was, as we were near Seapoint which, unknown to us, was on the Atlantic side of the Cape.

The next day we sailed off to make a stop at Port Elizabeth where we had a whole day to go ashore. We went to a place called Happy Valley where a stream came down to the sea and where the valley had been made lovely with gardens and a pavilion and tea house. By the roadside we found a young man selling oranges by the 'pocket'. We wanted to buy some, but did not know how many were in a 'pocket'. However, as they were very cheap by our standards, we bought a 'pocket' and were amazed to receive a sack full.

The next stop up the coast was at East London, where we were not to stay for very long. A young lady had travelled on the ship and we all knew that she was coming out to join her husband. As the ship docked, we could see a lone figure waiting on the quayside and a big cheer went up as she finally stepped ashore into his waiting arms. I often wondered how they fared.

We set off on the final lap to Durban, the landfall there not as dramatic as that of Cape Town. We had been passing along the coast for some time, and at last beyond a high hill, which we later discovered was called the Bluff, we saw the town and the docks appearing and I hastened to the cabin to do our last-minute packing and to retrieve the last of the drying washing from the laundry room. I returned to our cabin to find a frantic Ron looking for me. We had docked and the port authorities would not let anyone leave the ship until they had found me. It appeared that as I had come in under their strict health regulations I would not be permitted to go any further until I had had a chest X-ray to confirm the severity, or otherwise, of my condition. And so, in the fierce January heat and humidity, I was bundled into a car and driven across town to be X-rayed, while Ron met up with Bram, who had come to meet us.

Eventually I was returned to the docks after they had decided I was not liable to infect the whole of the South African population, and our exhausted party were able to pile into Bram's car and begin our journey inland.

I sat in the back of the car with the two fractious children, who, before long, fell into an exhausted sleep. It was not long before I joined them and so I have no memory of the long uphill drive out of Durban up the winding road into the hills. I vaguely remember being told that to our right was the Valley of a Thousand Hills and occasional brief stops for petrol and a bite to eat. Night falls about 7 p.m. in both summer and winter in South Africa, so the majority of our journey was in darkness and as we had to travel for over 400 miles and climb two high escarpments to reach the height of 6,000 feet above sea level onto the Highveld, it was the early hours of the morning before we approached the Witwatersrand, the range of hills on which Johannesburg stood. I roused myself and tried to peer into the darkness ahead at the long low skyline, where, as I watched, lightning flickered backwards and forwards along the horizon as a summer storm rumbled across the area.

At last we were driving through the deserted streets on the outskirts of the city which seemed to be a jumble of warehouses and factories until we reached the suburbs and finally drew up outside a low bungalow whose covered stoop shone with light, and inside was Margery waiting to welcome us. We unloaded our cases and attempted to do justice to the meal she had prepared for us which was laid out in the dining room, which also served as the entrance hall to the house. Then we were shown our room and after settling the children, collapsed into bed. We had arrived. We were in South Africa.

9

The following day we prepared to start our new life. Bram and Margery's house was at the top of a hill at the edge of the southern suburb of Forest Hill. A little further up the hill was an enormous concrete water tower and beyond it the hills fell away without any habitation. The road winding along the edge of the housing was called, for some reason, Rifle Range Road, no doubt a reminder of more warlike times. The house itself was set foursquare in a small garden with a short path leading to the covered stoop and its brilliant red polished floor. A screen door could be latched, leaving the front door open to make a cool through draft to the rest of the house. On one side of the entrance-cum-dining room was a small lounge and an archway led through at the back to a passageway, leading on the left to the kitchen. To the right, at the far end was the bathroom, with the main bedroom at the front of the house and two smaller bedrooms at the back. We had been warned about the earth tremors, but we got the fright of our lives during our first week there, when, in the middle of the night, there was a huge bang, the room shuddered and a long low rumble shook us in our beds. We were to become quite used to this phenomenon and soon took it in our stride. Very little damage ever ensued from these tremors, though we never knew what caused them. It may have been the extensive mine workings or just the geological fault on which the town was laid.

Summer storms were another matter and could be quite terrifying. We had arrived at the height of summer and the rarefied Highveld air would become sultry and hot as the afternoon wore on, until, at about five o'clock, just as all the office workers left for home, the heavens would open with torrential downpours and the thunder and lightning would reverberate among the high-rise office blocks. It was not unusual to see the young girls take off their shoes and run barefoot through the water. In the suburbs, deep storm-water drains ran along the sides of the road to catch the sudden influx of water and it was not unheard of for small animals, or even children, to be swept away in the torrents.

Ron was introduced to the engineering company where he would be employed as a fitter and turner, and he set off every day to catch the bus into town. I took the children out for walks and one day got talking with a lady who ran a children's nursery on Rifle Range Road. She invited me in for tea and we became quite friendly and I visited her often. She and her husband were due to leave for a long holiday in England and she asked if my husband and I would care to move into her home to look after it while they were away. I talked it over with Ron but we were keen to have our own home and we had looked at some flats which were being built a few streets away from Margery. With hindsight, I regretted turning her down as a few months without any overheads would have given us a better start, but soon we moved into our two-bedroom flat. Ron's mother lived lower down the hill in an older flat in Rosettenville and she and my father-in-law seemed to have settled in well. It was wonderful to us to be able to buy whatever food we needed, as many things had still been rationed when we left England. The range of fruits was incredible, things like peaches and apricots had been unobtainable or too expensive before, but now they could be bought for next to nothing. Sweetcorn became a favourite dish and meat was plentiful, good quality and cheap.

I decided to get a job and found places at a nursery school for Anne and Paul. I went for several interviews, but as I hadn't much experience of office work I was finding it difficult. Eventually I was taken on as a receptionist at an optician's in Johannesburg called Wolfson and De Wet. The owner was Mr Wolfson and there was no Mr De Wet, but he used the name to appeal to his Afrikaner customers. Mr Wolfson was a middle-aged Jewish gentleman with a very reserved manner who soon showed me the ropes, but the names of his customers had a nightmarish quality for me as I had never come across any like them before – Bezuidenhout, Groenevald, Van Skalkveik, Friekart, Van de Westhuizen and many more which I have now forgotten. Van de Merve was the Afrikaans' equivalent of Smith or Jones so it was important to get the first names right, and usually that was another minefield. Otherwise the job only entailed making appointments on the phone, sending out reminders and writing out the invoices. Ron had looked around for a better job and went to work for a man who was planning to manufacture a floor-polishing machine. The Progress Floor Polisher was an American-made machine and Ron was employed to redraw its parts sufficiently to take it out of reach of its patent. He had to travel around the Rand and get the various parts made and then set up an assembly line and employ the staff to put it into production. Of course, once he had done all that, his services were no longer required.

As a city, Johannesburg was very young. After gold was discovered on the Reef during the mid-1800s, it suffered the same fate as many other prospecting towns. A city of tents arose, saloons and brothels quickly followed, and it was only when the Big Boys moved in and set up large mining operations that civic pride took over, and streets were laid out neatly either north to south or east to west and named after the worthier citizens. So now there was a grid of main streets, the main ones being Eloff Street (north to south) and Commissioner Street (east to west), with lesser streets fanning out from them. Despite the earth tremors, buildings were mostly tall but local planning insisted that the foundations should be deep and provided the necessary car parking for the staff using them. There was a fine city hall and, across the intervening gardens, a library and museum. There were several attractive parks and a railway station with a splendid fountain in its entrance hall. The trains were on a lower level to the station and it seemed that this was due to a terrible explosion which had occurred when a train laden with explosives for the mines erupted and blew a huge hole in the area. This was later used to advantage in building the station over the gap. The art gallery was sited in Joubert Park.

A wide selection of department stores and other shops was on offer, Woolworths being the South African equivalent of Marks and Spencers. Ansteys was for the more upwardly mobile, while the O.K. Bazaars was a value-for-money shop which sold everything. A sign at the bottom of the escalators read, 'Bare-footed persons please use the stairs'. This of course referred to the Africans who were free to come and go in the shops during the day, but who had to leave the town at night and return to the townships. It took a little time to get used to the many black faces, and the suburb where we lived housed many 'girls' in the servants' quarters at the back of even the most modest of houses. 'Boyfriends' were not allowed to live in, but many did on the quiet, as the multitude of back-carried babies testified to. One had to appreciate their joy in living; one New Year's Day several were dancing in the street to the music of a wind-up gramophone perched on the head of a dancing fat momma. It wasn't unusual to see a man riding his bicycle wearing shorts, no socks and bicycle clips on his legs, the ensemble being completed by a radio aerial attached to the front handle of the bike.

On our first Sunday there we went down the hill to the small Salvation Army Corps at Rosettenville where Bram

126

played in the band. We were duly welcomed and worshipped there on a fairly regular basis. I did not have any strong feelings one way or another about Christianity, but I enjoyed the singing and the playing of the band. Sometimes we went to the main Corps of Johannesburg City on Commissioner Street where they had a very fine band and songsters. Ron seemed to be happy to become a part of that life again and I had no objections to going along with it. Most of the people who attended were first-generation immigrants, some of whom had come in under the assisted scheme held some years before but which was not now available. The Langs came from Plymouth and still spoke with their Devon drawl. Clarrie and Margaret Smith were stalwarts; Margaret never lost her Scottish accent until her dying day, and Clarrie was the smartest flag bearer in the Southern Hemisphere. Many of the officers were sent out from England, but there was a training college in Johannesburg which was laying the foundations for a South African-based staff. There was one Afrikaner who stood out from the rest, Brigadier (as he was then) Von Kleist and his wife.

Ron was asked if he would like to take charge of a small Corps at Bez (Bezuidenhout) Valley, where a thriving youth group needed a leader. He was given the rank of envoy, a non-commissioned rank, and largely unpaid, and he thoroughly enjoyed himself. However, he knew even better than I did that he wasn't supposed to smoke, but he continued to do so. We had left the flat in the southern suburbs and rented a house on the upper slopes of Bez Valley. It was similar in layout to Margery's house and in the kitchen was a large black wood-burning stove and above it a water cylinder to heat the water for the house. We were still very 'green' newcomers, and when, in the time-honoured manner, the next door 'girl' asked if we wanted someone to work for us, we happily took on her niece. She was young and very shy and didn't speak a great deal of English. One night, I had been waiting for Ron to come home as I needed some things from the shop, so before we left in the car I asked the girl to light the fire to heat up the water. The sudden darkness came down while we were out and when we returned it was to find that she had lit candles and placed them all around the house. She had never seen electric light before and was amazed when we showed her the switches. In the kitchen, the stove was burning merrily, and collected on the top of it was the tin bath filled with water and any other receptacle she had been able to find. Obviously a circulating water system was another eye-opener for her. It made me realise the great gap in our cultures, but she was a good, willing lass until she decided to return to her home. The next girl we had used to entertain, unknown to us, any passing punter until one night her husband came and made a bonfire of her clothes in our back garden. A quick call to the police soon sorted that out and we found another girl.

Our first Christmas was so strange to us, with the blazing sunshine and fierce summer heat. We had not got round to buying a fridge then, something that was unheard of in England, but when the turkey I had bought and cooked was uneatable the following day, we made sure that was our next purchase.

News came that Ron's younger brother Tom, his wife Iris and their little girl, Karen, had decided to come out to South Africa as well. At the same time, his younger sister Miriam with her husband Ronnie and their little daughter Janet were to travel on the same boat. Margery rented a house across the road from her, a strange place with myriad interlocking rooms, and she whitewashed the whole of the interior for the two families to share. It was never going to work for long of course, and they each went their separate ways. Tom, a toolmaker, soon found work and Ronnie got a job as a stationery salesman.

We had bought a small car and soon we were enjoying

outings to places such as Gillooley's Farm, a large area of wooded grounds where the children could roam free. Another favourite was a huge swimming pool south of the city, and trips to Pretoria just north of the city were also full of interest. The road wound along under eucalyptus trees and at one part, beaded African Ndbele women would sell their wares by the roadside. Just before reaching the city, the road off to the left led to the impressive Voortrekker Monument set on a hillside overlooking the town and facing the Union Buildings on a hillside in the far distance. The difference between the architecture spelled out the opposing cultures of the white community. The Voortrekker Monument was an austere structure, very tall and enshrining an enormous granite cenotaph on which was inscribed 'Ons vir jou Suid-Afrika'. The plaque was so positioned that each year at noon on 16 December, the anniversary of the Battle of Blood River, sunlight struck the inscription. Surrounding this huge edifice was a circular wall with carvings of Voortrekker wagons on it signifying the manner in which the settlers would draw themselves into a 'laager' or defensive ring at night-time during the Great Trek.

On the other hand, the Union Buildings, commissioned by the South African authorities in 1910 and designed by Sir Herbert Baker, nestled into the brow of the hill with graceful Renaissance columns. Below flowed terraces with lawns, fountains and waterfalls down to a wide grassy area at the foot.

Bez Valley was very steep and at the bottom of the roads there was a huge dip and then a sharp rise over the storm drains at the bottom. One day I was in the back of the car with the children when Ron went roaring down the road, forgetting the bump at the bottom. In those days before seat belts were thought of, as he soared over the bump, my head hit the roof of the car and I fell back stunned. When we got home I went to lie down on the bed, and a little later, when Ron came in to see how I was, I found that I knew what I wanted to say, but the sounds that came from my mouth didn't make any sense. I was panic stricken, and no matter how hard I tried, I could say nothing that could be understood. Ron calmed me down and I went back to sleep and later when I woke up I had returned to normal, but had a dreadful headache for the rest of the day. I imagine I must have suffered a minor cerebral haemorrhage, but was lucky that it dispersed with no untoward effects.

Ron was still working on the Progress floor polisher and things were looking very good for us. Anne was attending a nursery school at the end of the road which she enjoyed. She managed to pick up the measles bug while there and both she and Paul were quite ill for a while but got over it well. I was longing to have another child, especially now that help was at hand in the house and with the laundry. I felt it would be lovely to have another little girl and to be able to spend more time with my child and to enjoy being a mother with a little less of the hard work. Ron was happy for us to have another baby so we tried to ensure that the birth date would be in June along with the other two. Perhaps we tried too hard, but it wasn't until Christmas had come and gone that I was at last pregnant again. During this time I had had to attend the Chest Clinic regularly for X-rays and check-ups, and when I told them I was pregnant, the jolly doctor there said he had the best prophylactic solution, a glass of water, not before, not after, but instead of. Fortunately my health was good and the high veldt altitude was proving to be what I needed. The year 1955 was full of promise.

I felt well and suffered very little morning sickness, but one day Ron came home to tell me that his job with the Progress Floor Polisher Company was at an end. I suppose we should have seen it coming, but it was a shock nonetheless. He began to look for other work but there seemed to be little about at that time until he heard of a job in a factory just outside Krugersdorp, a small town to the west of Johannesburg. As it would be too far to travel we were able to rent a house on an estate near Leopardsvlei called Kenmare. Tom and Iris decided to come and join us with Karen, who was just a toddler. On the day that we moved in, Iris was very sick and it was thought that she might have a stomach ulcer. The next day she felt a little better and Tom went off to see if he could find work at one of the local factories. The children were fractious and just when it all began to feel a bit too much, a lorry rolled up on the unmade road outside filled with a gang of black workers. They were joined by a truck laying down tarmac then another spreading grit on top, at which the line of black workers picked up their brooms and, spread across the road, proceeded to sweep in the grit, all the while chanting and singing rhythmically. I am sure they were quite unaware of the row of fascinated little faces glued to the glass of the windows; it certainly was a godsend for two distracted mothers and for us it was an insight into how things were done in our adopted country. The houses were single storey, as was usual in South Africa, and were situated on good-sized plots. We had found one which had just been completed for a couple who had subsequently divorced; it had three bedrooms with a spacious living room and kitchen. We had only a small amount of furniture and we soon settled in. Anne and Paul were fascinated to find that the children who lived next door ran around barefooted and came in demanding that they too should go out and play without shoes. Off they came and out they went, but soon they were back in because their feet hurt so much. Our back yard had no lawn and the ground was hard on their tender little feet. Before many weeks had passed, however, they had toughened up, and along with all the other South African children, they ran around barefooted except when attending school or going into town with me. Unfortunately, Tom was unable to find any work in

Krugersdorp and he and Iris soon returned to Johannesburg where he found a good job as a toolmaker and they were able to rent a flat.

Krugersdorp was a good-sized town which was very Afrikaner in its set-up, but it had been swollen by some of the mining activity nearby and was a bustling little place with a Carnegie Library and impressive civic buildings. The Municipal outdoor swimming pool was a delight, with beautiful lawns around it and a fine pool.

The job that Ron had been offered did not materialise, however, and he arranged an interview with another company which was to take place in Johannesburg. We went on the train and I visited Margery while he went into the city. He was away for a very long time and eventually I got a phone call to meet him in town. I caught the bus and got to our meeting point to find that he was very much the worse for drink. Furiously we made for the railway station and the train back to Krugersdorp, my heart sinking as I worried about what we would do. He shut himself in the toilet as I comforted the tired children and I had to hammer on the door to rouse him as we approached Leopardsvlei station. He stumbled out and was in no condition to help me with Anne and Paul. It was a long walk to our home and the short cut took us along the industrial railway, deserted at that time of night. I had never known such despair with two small children, another on the way and a husband who had suddenly turned into a stranger.

We finally reached home and went to bed and the next day he was full of apologies, but suddenly our rosy future no longer stretched ahead of us. Eventually he found a job as a manager at a large factory, but only after two months with no income. We owed our rent and I eked out what money we had to feed us. It was then that I discovered how most people lived: the secret was to open accounts at the shops with which we dealt, so I had a grocery account at the local shop, another at the chemist and one at a store in Krugersdorp called Greatermans. When we were living at Bez Valley, I had found that the prices for children's clothes were very high, so Ron had bought me a hand-operated Singer sewing machine. I bought material and a pattern and made my first little dress for Anne, a pretty pink cotton with short sleeves. After that there was no stopping me and I made shirts and trousers for Paul and had soon attempted dresses for myself. Greatermans sold materials and so I could pick up remnants cheaply to keep us clothed.

Winter was under way and the days were dry and cold in the morning, heating up to a pleasant warmth by midday then plunging to near freezing once darkness fell. I went to the local clinic in town for my ante-natal checks and was put in touch with a midwife who would come and deliver the baby at home when the time came. She gave me a list of items to buy and after the rent arrears had been settled and the bills paid, I gradually gathered together what I would need. We had put a deposit on a pram at a shop in Johannesburg and finally had the money to go and collect it. I suspected that Ron still took a drink after work, but there had been no recurrence of the dreadful train journey. I could not be angry with him for long as he would go to great lengths when he was sober to do all he could, and he surprised me one day by travelling into Jo-burg and returning on the train with the pram that we had put to one side. Somehow the love we had for each other was strong enough to see us through, but I was constantly aware that things could easily go badly wrong.

We began to make friends with some of our neighbours; Hennie and Jan lived next door, an English-speaking but Afrikaans couple. Jan was very withdrawn but Hennie and I got on well. They had their first little boy and Hennie had a devoted maid called Peggy who had looked after her all her life. Franz and Thora lived across the road in an older house. They had two little girls, one a bit older than Anne and one younger. Franz was Scottish and Thora was an English-speaking girl from Durban, where her mother still lived. I used to be green with envy when they would pack up their car and set off to stay with her mother for two weeks. Peg and Ray lived a couple of streets away; they came from the Midlands, and Ray was a large red-faced fellow while Peg was tall and wiry. They had an older son and a daughter about Anne's age.

I wrote to my aunts in England as often as I could and had lots of letters from them, but I never felt the dreadful homesickness that came to many English girls. The perceived wisdom was that a homesick wife should be packed off back to the UK for a holiday and then she would soon see how much better off she was in South Africa. Even in those days, public transport in South Africa was strictly segregated and one young wife was mortified back in England when a Jamaican boarded the bus she was on and her small son piped up in a loud voice, 'Mummy, what is that Kaffir doing on our bus?' We were always careful to see that our own children learned to respect everyone whatever their colour and in a country where everyone had a servant, our children were never allowed to give orders to anyone working for us.

Margery was very active in the Salvation Army in Johannesburg and was good at putting on dramas. She talked Ron into taking the part of Christ in one of her productions and he would travel in for rehearsals. As the time came nearer for the opening I became frantic as I was aware that he didn't know his lines very well and I would stand over him feeding him his cues and trying to get him to take it seriously. But with his usual air of confidence he told me not to worry. We all went to the performance where much of the action took place with Ron seated at a table. I was mortified when I heard the lady in front of me whisper to her companion, 'He's reading the script!' And indeed he was, but with his usual charm he seemed to get away with it.

10

It was time to call the midwife and a few hours after I had settled the children into bed, labour proceeded to its climax. As the pains reached their zenith the midwife asked if I wanted an increase in the gas and air and gratefully I accepted. The next thing I knew Ron was bending over me and saying, 'It's a little boy!' Groggily I asked, 'How do you know, I haven't had it yet!' But indeed it was, a little seven-pounder who had arrived with the cord wrapped around his neck, but all that had been dealt with while I was unconscious and although he was a little blue in the face, he soon pinked up and after a wash down I was settled back into my own bed. Next morning Ron woke Anne and Paul up and brought them to see their new baby brother. Anne was enthralled but Paul, at just turned three, was not amused. We decided to call him Christopher and William after my father.

Finances were still difficult and we were startled when the midwife had gathered up her belongings and with arms folded expected to be paid on the spot. We did not have the money and later we had a nasty letter from her saying, 'Poor baby, two weeks old and not paid for,' so somehow Ron found the money. Probably borrowed it, I expect. Finance was dire and we were still struggling to catch up after paying off the debts we had incurred when he had been out of work for so long. It was not unusual to receive threatening letters and when Ron told me, in what was meant to be a reassuring tone, that, 'if the bailiffs come to take our goods, the law says they cannot take our beds,' I realised that something would have to be done. There was no way I could depend upon my husband to take charge of our family income, he just did not understand the importance of paying our way and was quite happy to wait and see what the morrow would turn up.

I started to look for ways to cut back our expenses and fortunately our friends Thora and Franz from across the road at number 24, Ardtully Street had decided to move and rent a better house around the corner. Franz, had a good job at the local paint factory, Plascon Paints, and so they could afford a nice ranch-style house at a higher rent. The rent of their old house was £15 a month, compared with the £20 we were paying, so when Christopher was a few weeks old, we moved to the house across the road.

It stood foursquare with a corrugated iron roof (not unusual at that time), with a wide flight of steps leading to the red-polished stoop with double glass doors opening into a small hall. Double doors on the left led into the lounge with a fireplace at the far end and in the far right-hand wall, double glass doors opened into the dining room at the back. The kitchen was through a door on the right, a large square room with fitted wooden cupboards along the back wall, a sink to the left, and facing into the back garden, a door onto a small verandah and steps leading down. Next to the back door was a window and in the corner a small coal- and wood-burning stove which heated the water in the cylinder above. There was just room for the refrigerator against the other wall, with a door leading into a dog leg of a passage with the bathroom and toilet on the left, the back bedroom straight ahead then round the corner a small bedroom on the left and the main bedroom at the front of the house. Another door on the right opened back onto the other side of the small hall at the front.

The floors were all wooden and polished to a high gleam. We took with us our 'girl' Nellie, a rotund little thing and very good natured. But soon she had to leave, and she introduced Emily, who was looking for work. Emily was a tall Zulu woman with much grace and a lovely manner. The children adored her and she settled into the girl's room built onto the back of the garage which was equipped with its own toilet. Everyone respected her privacy and on the odd occasion when I needed to enter her room, I was impressed with the way she kept it. The single iron bedstead was raised up on bricks and was always covered by a spotless white embroidered cloth. Beside her bed was a cupboard also covered by an embroidered cloth and along one wall a rail was used to hang her clothes. We provided her with a uniform consisting of a deep blue overall and white aprons, and with her food, which was a large bag of mealie meal once a month and the meat that Zulus like and which was bought specially for them at the butcher's. This was meat with plenty of bone in it and in the afternoons after she had lit the stove for the evening hot water, she would use her own pan to cook her evening meal on it. It was her main meal of the day; other than that, she had unlimited tea with lots of sugar and thick-cut slices of bread at midday. On top of that she received £5 per month, which was more disposable income than I ever had!

Servants were not allowed to have their husbands living in white areas but everyone turned a blind eye to any nocturnal comings and goings, and in the course of time, Emily became pregnant. She continued to work for us at her own request and when the news came that she had had her baby at the local hospital, we gladly went to collect her and bring her back home. I shall never forget arriving at the hospital and a nurse wheeling a trolley towards us covered by a blanket. On whipping this off we were treated to the sight of a whole row of little black babies all tightly swaddled and blinking in the sudden light. Fortunately Emily was able to identify hers and we took them back home with us. We insisted she rest for a while but she was soon back working with her baby snugly swaddled and tucked up on her back.

An ancient van toured the estate every week owned by a little Indian called Mr Patel, who sold us our fresh vegetables. The native girls all called him Sammy and we learned that the doctor who attended the black people, also an Indian, was known to them as 'the Sammy Doctor' and he it was who presided at the native hospital.

These were the days when polio was rampant. We met a Dutch couple who lived nearby. They had emigrated from Holland and the husband told us that during the war he worked in the Resistance in Holland. He said that when the raid on Arnhem was imminent, he and his friends discovered that the Germans were expecting it and they tried, unsuccessfully as it happened, to warn the Allies of this. They had two sons, and we heard later that both had contracted polio, and as one child was wheeled out having died, the other was wheeled in. He was treated in an iron lung and fortunately survived. Everyone was terrified of the infection and our children were forbidden to buy ice creams from the boys on three-wheeler bikes who circled the estate.

We asked Margery to dedicate Christopher at the small Salvation Army Citadel in Krugersdorp and invited the whole family. I baked for the occasion, but in the event, only Margery turned up. Apparently we were *persona non grata*. Tom and Iris continued to be frequent visitors, however, and we always had a large bonfire and fireworks in the back garden to celebrate Guy Fawkes, much to the consternation of our Afrikaner neighbours.

I no longer had to attend the chest clinic as I had been declared clear of TB and my temporary visa was exchanged for permanent residence. However, for many years afterwards I made sure that I had an annual check up and X-ray. I was concerned that I was unable to breast feed Christopher; when Anne was born and taken away from me for six weeks I had been given drugs to dry up my milk and had hoped to be able to breast feed Paul. But it was not deemed safe for me and so he had been bottle fed as well. This was no big problem as the dried milk and orange juice came free at the clinic, but I was very keen to at last do my bit in Christopher's case. Shortly after we had moved across the road, I found that I lost my milk every time I took a bath, and that the amount I had available became less and less. This was a disaster in our straightened circumstances, as the SMA dried milk was expensive and our bill at the chemist shot up. As soon as possible I began to wean him in the days when convenient jars of baby food were not available. Starting with porridge, in a few weeks he was successfully downing sieved pumpkin and squash padded out with potato.

As the warmer weather came with the approach of Christmas, we would spend our weekends at the Municipal swimming pool where our two eldest soon took to the water like little seals. There was a good-sized children's pool with shallow steps leading into it, and Christopher loved to play with the jets of water methodically squirting out of the pipe along the top. When held on his back by his shoulders he would scissor his legs like a frog and delight in the splashes he made. Most mornings involved coffee at the house of one or other of our friends while our children played in the garden. We had another old car, a little larger than our last one, and we enjoyed exploring the countryside to the west of the town. The high veldt dropped down by several thousand feet to an area around Rustenburg in the Magaliesberg hills where, for the first time, we saw oranges growing on the trees. They were a winter fruit and their large orange globes hung suspended among the deep green foliage. On one estate, an ostrich strode along the high wire fence, much to our astonishment. In Rustenburg itself we were amused to find a signpost in the middle of town pointing out the direction and the distances to dozens of places from the Cape to Cairo.

The Pines was also a favourite weekend spot to visit. Situated down a corrugated dirt road, it nestled in a small valley surrounded by pine and gum trees. There was a huge swimming pool and at the far end, a shallower children's paddling pool with grassy terraces sloping down towards the water. We went there one day when Christopher was just a few weeks old. His pram was also a carry cot and we settled it onto one of the terraces and proceeded to unpack our picnic and spread out the rugs. Suddenly there was a shout and commotion at the water's edge and we turned around to see Paul being lifted out of the water. He had mistaken the deep end of the swimming pool for the shallow children's end and had leapt in while our attention had been diverted. Fortunately a young man saw what had happened and, diving in fully clothed, brought him to the surface before any damage was done. Ron took the young man to our home to dry off and gave him a set of clothing to replace his own wet outfit. We felt it was the least we could do. This was not to be the last time that our eldest son diced with death.

I still corresponded with our friends Cynthia and Val whom we had met on the boat coming out. Cynthia wrote to tell me of a trip they had taken to South West Africa from their home in Cape Town. It sounded wonderful and I was full of envy at the idea of the two of them just packing up what they needed for themselves and taking off. Even the shortest expedition of ours involved prams, nappies, damp face cloths, bottles and changes of clothes and sometimes felt like preparing for an Arctic expedition. But I should not have been envious because the sad truth was that Cynthia had been unable to fall pregnant. A ruptured appendix and peritonitis in her teens had made a hash of her internal organs. One day a letter came to tell us that the insurance company that Val worked for was to relocate to Johannesburg, so soon they were settled in a house on a new development, Roosevelt Park, in the northern suburbs of Johannesburg. It was good to have their company again as we all got on well. Ron was always the centre of attention in any company with his quirky sense of humour and fun-loving nature, so we always had plenty of friends. While he still liked to drink, and sometimes overdid it, things were on an even keel to a large extent. I had persuaded him to let me run our bank account after he had proved again and again that to him, a bank account gave him unlimited access to the bank's resources, and this couldn't go on. South Africa was very male orientated and I found it amusing, and if truth be told, a bit annoying, that I had to have my husband's permission to open a bank account. Little did they realise what a good turn I was doing them.

Such tranquillity did not last. There was a terrible accident at the factory where Ron was manager and safety officer; a worker fell into a boiling vat and was killed. The company began to question Ron about his references – goodness knows what he had told them when he applied for the job – but they were not satisfied and he was out of work again. I would buy the newspapers, the *Star* and the *Rand Daily Mail* and go through the vacancy columns with him. He had decided to go for a salesman's job instead of working in a factory as there were benefits such as a company car and such a job would certainly suit his temperament with his ability to get on with people. The drinking started again, however. Apparently, when he was supposedly out looking for work he was a regular at a local pub called the Witpoortjie Arms. South African pubs were very rough and ready, a hang over from the early mining days, and a place where respectable women never went. This came to light when the chemist's bill arrived one day and I saw that it included invoices for a number of expensive films. I immediately went to the shop to question this and was mortified to be shown a copy of the invoice with Ron's signature on it. I realised that, being short of ready cash, he had hit on the idea of taking the films down to the pub and selling them. Of course I tackled him about it and we had a terrible row. I thought he had learned his lesson but it seemed I couldn't trust him.

There seemed to be only one way for me to ensure that we kept a roof over our heads and had food on the table; I would have to get a job myself.

I knew I could depend on Emily and that the children would be in good hands. Anne had started school almost a year before and Paul was just about to begin. Christopher was eleven months old. I wondered what my options were. I had done some office work for my father and had taught myself to type with two fingers, but that would never do. I had nursing experience but had not taken my finals, so that would have to suffice. I enquired at the local hospital but they had no vacancies. They suggested I try at the Discoverers Hospital nearer to Johannesburg in a place called Florida and I went for an interview and was taken on as an assistant nurse. Not a high salary but enough to cover any shortfalls in whatever Ron was able to provide.

The hospital was a small provincial one with two floors, men on the ground floor and women upstairs. A mix of medical and surgical work was done and I was appointed to work on the women's ward. Most of the staff were Afrikaners, which was not a great barrier as everyone was bilingual. The schools were either exclusively English or Afrikaans speaking but in each, the other language was taught, so it was not unusual for people to swap over from one language to the other, often mid-sentence. I was lucky enough to team up with another assistant nurse called Lisa Swannepoel who was an Afrikaner but preferred to speak English. We would laugh and joke together as we worked and she would say 'We Koekemoors' always do this or that, which we found amusing for some reason. I soon learned the Afrikaans for sheet and blanket – 'larkin' and 'comber' respectively – and found I could understand a great deal of what was said, even if I could speak very little. This came in very useful when I realised that some of the other nurses would make derisory comments about me, thinking I did not understand. I was

143

soon able to let them know in English that I understood only too well, and I had no more trouble.

It was a strange situation that we found ourselves in, as for us the memories of the Second World War were vivid and still, to a great extent, hung over us, so at first it was some time before we realised that these events had largely passed the Southern African continent by. Certainly many troops had passed through the country and Simonstown was a British naval base, but most Afrikaners, if asked, would have said that their sympathies lay with the Germans and it was English-speaking South Africans who joined the British forces.

Not only that, but we soon discovered that the Boer War was of far more recent interest to the Afrikaners, while we, although we knew it had taken place, knew few of the details. Indeed, when we were told of the concentration camps where the British imprisoned the families of the Boer fighters, we found it hard to believe. There was still much bitterness and so being English made me a target for some venom.

Many of the patients were Afrikaner women, or 'tannies'. They were renowned for their cooking prowess and it often showed when we had the task of bed-bathing ladies whose fat thighs almost overflowed over the bed edges. A 'tannie' was an 'auntie', 'oom' was an 'uncle', and these were accepted terms to use even though no relationship existed. Maternity and gynae cases were also treated and I remember one lady who had miscarried. She was distraught as they would not tell her what sex her child would have been. So I promised to see what I could do, and in the sluice found the foetus in a kidney dish waiting to be disposed of. I was able to tell her it would have been a boy although I would have been in serious trouble if I had been discovered, but I knew that in her place I would have wanted to know.

Another disturbing case was a woman who had taken tablets to end her life. She was still alive but unconscious and her anxious family gathered around her bed in a side ward for most of a day before she finally found the release she had sought.

One day a young woman came in for a D and C, a not uncommon operation sometimes used in cases of heavy menstrual bleeding. However, it soon became apparent there was more to it than that as she made no secret of the fact that she, the wife of the local chemist, was the lover of one of the doctors, and that *his* wife was now an item with her husband. This, it turned out, was an abortion, not a D and C, illegal at that time, but under the auspices of the medical fraternity, it was quietly 'seen to'.

I found I was having a lot of trouble when making beds as it was painful to lift my arms above my shoulders. I reported this to the sister, who sent me to see the hospital physiotherapist. She arranged for me to have my back massaged where, with fingers that felt like iron bars, she discovered and kneaded lumps in the muscles around my shoulder blades. The first few sessions were agonising, but eventually I got back the full movement in my arms and thereafter had no more trouble.

I had started work in August just as the South African winter was reaching its climax. It had taken us some time to come to grips with our new climate, used as we were to the vagaries of an English one where all four seasons could be experienced in the course of a week. Winters on the high veld were bitterly cold in the mornings, with hard frosts, but by midday, temperatures would reach 20°C. Additionally, from June there would be no rainfall, everything would dry up and the air would be full of static electricity. Climbing in and out of a car often resulted in a nasty shock from the door handle and many cars trailed a piece of chain at the back to earth the car. Then in August the winds would come and the dust would fly from unmade roads and from the tops of the mine dumps, making it almost impossible to keep a house dust free. In September the storm clouds gathered and the welcome rain would damp down all the dust. Temperatures rose and the daily tropical storm would pour down in the late afternoon on most days. Sometimes the storms arrived after the children had gone to bed, and as our house had a corrugated iron roof, if hailstones came, the noise could be deafening. And so we would wake the children and bring them through to the lounge. There we would open up the curtains, stand them on the sofa and give a big cheer at every bolt of lightning and roll of thunder. To this day they all enjoy a good storm and have no fear. The storms could be dangerous though; natives sheltering under trees and golfers caught out on the links were often victims of lightning strikes and small animals could be beaten to death and cars badly dented by the force of the hailstones.

One day the children came home saying that their friends parents were giving away their dog and could they please have her. Kleinjie – pronounced clinekee – the Afrikaans for 'little one', was a cute little dachshund who became a firm favourite. However, she had not been spayed and we were warned to keep her in when she came into season. We were also offered the services of a male dachshund owned by the same people when the time was right. In time the young dog was introduced to Kleinjie and they seemed to get on well, but after a day or two she managed to escape into the waiting paws of a scruffy little terrier who had been waiting his chance. Kleinjie's pregnancy progressed smoothly and we made up a comfortable bed for her beside the stove in the kitchen. One evening after the children had gone to bed, she came whining to me and we realised her time had come. As the pups started to arrive, we roused the children to come and watch as each little bundle arrived as though wrapped up in cellophane. Kleinjie knew what to do, however, and with her teeth released them one by one and nudged them towards her belly. There were four, one dog and three bitches.

146

Then started the busiest time of that little dog's life. She was a devoted mother, cleaning and feeding them, barely leaving them to care for her own needs, and she raised them all perfectly. Eventually homes were found for them all despite their lack of pedigree; in fact, some years later a lady came to ask if we had any more.

The Rand Easter show was a great annual event held on a large sloping space to the north of Johannesburg. It was part Ideal Homes Exhibition, part farming events such as sheep dog trials and also a wonderful fair with a huge ferris wheel. The grounds were approached up a wide avenue at the top of which was a swirling glittering mirrored ball and although I hated heights I was prevailed upon by the children to go up on the wheel. From the top the view was stupendous all the way to the Magaliesberg Hills and across the vista of mine dumps and over the skyscrapers of downtown Johannesburg. Companies came from all around the world to show their products at this fair, as the country was thriving and business was good. On our first visit we came across a stall demonstrating Necchi sewing machines and I was enthralled at their versatility as the machinist did embroidery and made buttonholes at the flick of a switch. So we paid our deposit and bought one and never was a machine put to such good use.

Although television was becoming the norm in England, here in South Africa it would be many years before it would put in an appearance. But we did enjoy the drive-in cinemas. The children would be bathed and put into their night clothes with cuddly toys and blankets in the back of the car and we would set off to the local drive-in. The cars were parked on a slight upward incline and the microphone was unhooked from the stand and attached inside the car, where we could sit in comfort and watch the latest film. One drive-in had been established on top of an old mine dump near the city centre and was one of the most popular.

147

Val's job with the insurance company came with a trip back to the UK every few years. On their first visit back 'home' they went to see Val's parents and Cynthia was incensed when, expecting to be asked all about their new life, they were smartly sat down in front of the television set and not allowed to interrupt whatever the programme was they were watching! Conversation obviously was an early casualty of television. They were keen to adopt a child but were told that they would be unable to as they were living abroad.

I then discovered that Ron was being made bankrupt as he had not kept up the payments on the sewing machine, the fridge and the few pieces of modest furniture that we owned. He had to go to court in Johannesburg and a firm of solicitors in Krugersdorp was appointed to whom he had to pay a certain sum every month and they undertook to make a disbursement to the various creditors. It was apparent that even the responsibility of these payments could not be left to Ron and that in order to cover them I would need to earn more money. Although the jobs that he got were good, with adequate salary and car, his earnings leached away as he took to brandy drinking, coming home most evenings late and obviously the worse for wear. I realised I would need extra skills in order to find an office job that would have more regular hours and would pay a better rate. At the end of our street across the road from the T-junction was the local high school and I got in touch with the teacher there who taught accountancy and bookkeeping. I paid him to come to our house and to teach me the rudiments of simple bookkeeping and accounts. Thus armed, I went into Johannesburg on my day off and registered with an employment agency. This was the accepted way of finding office work and the deal was that they were paid a large proportion of the first month's salary. As I was not bilingual, work would have to be in Johannesburg as Krugersdorp was largely

Afrikaans and I would have to travel either by train, or, if he was in work, get a lift from Ron. There was an excellent train service which stretched along the whole of the Reef, as the mining area was called. Gold had been discovered in the hills of the Witwatersrand along a stretch of many miles, the centre of which was Johannesburg, and trains ran to the east as far as Springs and in the west, went beyond Krugersdorp as far as Randfontein. They ran frequently and were of course for the use of whites only. The black population had good train services out to the various 'locations'. At one point on the journey into town, we passed over a deep valley which was filled with a shanty town, which, in the early morning, was filled with the smoke from the fires lit to cook the morning breakfast. Later, Father Trevor Huddlestone would make this his area of confrontation, but it was already an area of concern for the authorities. Despite the pass system, which was designed to control the number of blacks leaving the rural areas to seek work in the city, many still poured in and lived in these makeshift dwellings erected out of corrugated iron and cardboard.

The employment agency sent me for an interview at a plumber's business situated in Jeppe, the stop before Johannesburg. S.G. Norman was a one-man business, the proprietor being S.G. Norman himself. He employed three plumbers and spent his own time going round the town drumming up business. The office was a ramshackle building opening straight off a side street with me in the front office and S.G. Norman, when he put in an appearance, in a smaller inner office. In the winter months it was so cold that I had an electric fire under my desk and aimed at my legs to keep me warm. There I took phone calls for jobs and gave them out to the plumbers as they phoned in when the last job was completed. S.G. Norman priced each job and I sent out the invoices, and at the end of the month, the statements. When the cheques came in, I sent out the receipts and did the banking, then chased up all the non-payers. It was not taxing work, and I also took calls for the two electricians who had premises next door.

The plumbers, and their black labourers, were a good crowd, and I did their wages as well. A man used to come into the office from time to time, begging for money for food, so I would give him a 'ticky', as a threepenny piece was called, to buy some chips at the shop across the road. One day Tommy, one of the plumbers, was in the office when he came in and I gave the man his ticky. Tommy said, 'You shouldn't do that as he will just spend it on drink.' I found it hard to believe as I didn't think anything could be bought for that amount, so Tommy told me to come to the office door and look up the street. We were just in time to see the man disappearing into the pub on the corner. Apparently a tot of malmsbury wine – like a heavy port – could be had for a ticky. So next time he came in – obviously I was a soft touch – I called the tea boy from the back of the office and gave him the ticky telling him to go to the chip shop and buy chips for this 'boss'. He did so, I handed them over and never saw the man again.

Things at home didn't get any better. The man I thought I knew had changed out of all recognition. Each night I went to bed in despair, but found that by the next morning I would be ready to face the world again. We were barred from taking on any hire-purchase agreements due to Ron's bankruptcy, and then I discovered post-dated cheques. Most firms would accept a sale at cash price if six post-dated cheques were used to pay for the goods. As I now had my own bank account we were able to buy some essentials by this method. The first purchase was a washing machine to make it a bit easier for Emily. I was also able to spend my evenings and weekends making clothes for myself and the children, and even leisure shirts for Ron.

The children were all blessed with good appetites and we

could eat quite cheaply. When the 'Sammy van' came to the door with his loads of vegetables, I would buy a 'ticky' of soup greens, a generous helping of all the ingredients for a good soup. That, along with some shinbone from the butcher made a nourishing stew padded out with dumplings. Vegetables were plentiful and I would buy pumpkins and squash and large sacks of gem squash. These were like green tennis balls with a hard shell and could be stored indefinitely. Emily cooked sweet potatoes by mashing them and mixing in green beans and for sweets we would have fruit salads with pineapple, banana and orange, flavoured with grenadilla. Guavas with custard were another favourite and there were never, ever, any table tantrums. In contrast, my friend Thora's two girls were a nightmare, every meal a battle with pleas from their mother 'just to eat a little, dear'. She would buy chicken, a luxury in those days, and still they would not be tempted. In desperation she even went so far as to 'borrow' my kids and invited them to a meal so that her two might get the message. Many years later Anne told me that sometimes, if there was something on their plates that they didn't like, they would hide it under the upturned gem squash outer casing.

One Saturday we planned to go for a day out and loaded the children into the car. As we were about ready to go, Ron said he had forgotten something and dashed back into the house. At the same time I realised that I hadn't packed any fruit to take with us and went in after him only to find him standing in the kitchen drinking vodka straight from a bottle he must have had concealed. I was horrified, and finally realised that there was a serious problem. After many arguments and promises by him to reform, I finally managed to get him to agree to attend an Alcoholics Anonymous meeting. At first all went well, but then the meetings were hijacked by a lady with Pentecostal leanings who spent the time uttering long and earnest prayers. I had no doubt of her sincerity, but it didn't help our situation.

New housing estates were springing up north of Johannesburg and one of our favourite outings was to go and look at show houses. How I longed for a home of my own and how galling it was to know that on Ron's earnings we could have well afforded it, if only he did not drink.

Anne and Paul attended the local English-speaking school and were making good progress. They caught a bus at the end of the road that took all the children direct to the school. I was at home on holiday on one occasion when two crestfallen little figures arrived back at the house after having been waved off half an hour before in good time for the bus. Unfortunately, so they said, the bus had been early and had left without them. I sensed a rat on the loose, and a little close questioning revealed that the plan had been to hide behind the bus shelter until the bus had gone and then come home in the hopes of a trip to the swimming pool, perhaps? Hopes were dashed as I got the car out and drove them to school, taking them in and apologising for their lateness.

11

Time was passing, the children were getting older and other events in our lives were about to bring about changes. One day a letter came from Auntie Ethel saying that if possible, she would like to come and visit us. I immediately wrote back and said we would be only too pleased to see her. Eventually she managed to book a berth on a Union Castle boat which would bring her round to Durban.

Meanwhile, Ron's parents had gone to be caretakers at a holiday home run by the Salvation Army at Doonside, just south of Durban. So we booked a holiday to coincide with our trip to Durban to meet Ethel from the boat. This was our first major holiday and we set off from home in the early hours of the morning while the air was still fresh and cool. The roads were clear at this hour and we made good time. As the sun rose on our left, the children looked out of the car window where it appeared that as we drove along, it was rolling along the horizon like a huge red ball. This optical illusion kept them fascinated for some time until we were able to stop for breakfast. But as the day progressed and the heat became more intense, it was a very fractious party which finally arrived at Doonside. Next morning none of us could wait to make our way to the beach, a delight which didn't come our way very often, living as we did so far from the sea.

The day came for the ship to dock at Durban. We got there early to have a good view of my aunt's arrival and took the precaution of engaging the services of a very large Zulu porter to assist with her trunks. Eventually the gang way was in place and we checked her cabin number at the purser's office, then made our way to her cabin. We found her in the throes of last-minute packing along with a formidable lady with whom she had shared the cabin. This lady was a frequent visitor apparently and had patronized my aunt in no uncertain manner. Spying our large Zulu she imperiously ordered him to come and take her trunk so it was with some quiet pleasure that we informed her that he was there to take my aunt's trunk, not hers. We left her suitably crestfallen to make her own arrangements and swept off the ship with Ethel.

We spent another week at Doonside before setting off once more for Johannesburg. Ethel settled in well with us and we had very pleasant outings at the weekends. Ron made an effort to be at home in the evenings and his drinking, while heavy, was not too excessive.

I felt that my time at S.G. Norman's was coming to an end and that I needed something more demanding. So I went to an employment agency once more and they sent me for an interview as a stock control clerk at the National Trading Company. I got the job and was soon well versed in the work. I had discovered that whatever job I took, each company had its own way of doing things, so with a modicum of intelligence it was possible to pick up the reins quite quickly.

The National Trading Company supplied all the sanitary ware for the huge townships being built to the west of the city – the townships which would become known as Soweto – short for South Western Townships. Consignments of 500 baths, basins, toilets and sinks would go out on a daily basis along with all the fiddly bits like u-bends, couplings and copper pipes. All the loads were listed on the invoices which then came to us where, seated before huge filing drawers, we would go through piles of documents and deduct the amounts from the listed stores. The busiest days were when fresh stocks arrived and had to be added onto the lists. The

154

yearly stocktaking was a nightmare; we did quite well apart from finding one bath unaccounted for, and despite our best efforts and many rechecks, we could not find it. No doubt an extra one had been added on to a truck at some point.

Cynthia and Val came home from another trip back to the UK with a new adopted baby daughter. It seemed that the law had been changed in England to allow adopted children to be taken to live in other countries and they were ecstatic. She was a lovely little thing and they felt at last they were a complete family. She was to be called Lynne and Cynthia wrapped her whole life around her.

I still felt that we were living on a knife edge in a situation that I was only barely coping with. To some extent, the fact that sunset occurred within a two-hour stretch, both winter and summer, meant that we no longer experienced the long summer evenings of Europe, nor the short winter days, so routine was fairly constant. Without the lure of television, the children listened to their favourite radio programmes and then bedtime came at a reasonable hour as the morning schedule started early, school beginning at 8 a.m. This meant that by and large they were unaware of the stresses and arguments caused by their father's drinking. However, I knew this could not last, and because my feelings for him were still strong, I did not want them to lose regard for their father.

A newspaper article seemed to provide a possible solution. Apparently some government schools had been set up in remoter regions as boarding schools for farming families, but they were finding that there weren't enough local children to fill them. Consequently they were to be made available to children living in more built-up areas and offered a good education to boarders in lovely surroundings. The one which was featured in the article was in the Northern Transvaal at a place called Henaetsburg in an area of rolling hills, forests and mountain streams. We got in touch with them and were

155

invited to go and see for ourselves, so, accompanied by Auntie Ethel, we drove north-east and checked into the Magoebaskloof Hotel. It was perched at the head of an enormous valley, and the view from our rooms at the back of the hotel was stupendous. This was the area supposedly given over to the Rain Queen of popular myth from the previous century, and one could well believe that she had functioned here as mists would sweep down over the forests and hidden lakes and streams. The hotel itself was somewhat run down but its magnificent situation more than made up for any deficiencies.

The next day we went to the school and were taken round to see all the buildings and to hear of the schedule of events there were for the children. The grounds were vast and well looked after and I felt that the children would be safe here. We booked them in to start at the beginning of the next term.

Auntie Ethel's stay was drawing to a close and we offered her the chance to go on a tour of the Kruger Park Game Reserve as we felt that having travelled so far to see us, she should at least have the opportunity to see some of the wildlife. But she said she preferred to spend the remaining time with us. However, we had been told of the mine dances held on a Sunday at the gold mines just off the Main Reef Road. The gold was mined by Africans who were contracted from tribes from all over southern Africa. Recruiting teams would go out to remote tribal lands and the young men would be recruited for a certain length of time. They were to live on the mines where hostels were provided and at the end of their span of duty, they would be returned home with sufficient money to buy the cattle which would ensure that they could purchase a wife, or even two or three, if they had done well. Cattle were their gold standard, as it were, and the system worked well. Every so often a dance would be held on the mine grounds and each tribe would compete and perform the dance traditional to their own tribe. Strangely, not many people were aware of this outstanding happening, or if they were, were not particularly interested. But we knew it was something Auntie Ethel would enjoy and would be a memory for her to take home with her.

So we booked our tickets and on the day, drove to the mine recreation grounds. The dances were held in a huge open-air auditorium with rough wooden seating all around. The white people were seated on the shady side and behind the 'orchestra' which was already warming up. This consisted of massive drums made out of metal oil barrels with skins stretched across them, and their reverberations pounded out and filled us with their sound. In front of them were the home-made xylophones, at least five or six, all played at top decibels in a cacophony of sound that had very little form or what we might consider 'music' attached to it. As we settled ourselves, the dusty circle was empty when, without any apparent signal, the music stopped. There was utter silence for a while, and then double doors over on the right-hand side were flung open and the first set of dancers entered. They came in in a long file as the drums and xylophones started up again. With black skins gleaming in the heat, they pranced their way across the hot sand, singing their monotonous chants with occasional yells. Team after team, one after another came all afternoon; some had feathers in their headdresses and attached to their elbows, some had bells strapped to their legs which they used to emphasise the rhythm of their dance. The Zulus came with their shields and short stabbing spears, lifting their legs in unison and stamping them on the ground, raising the dust above them. I doubt if it would have been possible to see such a sight anywhere else on the African continent where so many tribes were gathered together.

We finally left exhausted and with the drum rhythm still pounding in our ears. A sight never to be forgotten.

Soon it was time for Auntie to leave, and we saw her off

at the station at Johannesburg where she was to catch a train for Cape Town from where her ship was to sail.

With Auntie gone and the two eldest children safely far away, things became bad again and Ron would regularly arrive home the worse for wear. Unwisely I would berate him and often he would erupt in violence. On one occasion I left the house and ran all the way through the industrial estate to the police station. But in those days, when Erin Pizzey, while perhaps not still a twinkle in her father's eye, was at least playing hopscotch in the school playground, I was advised to go home and make it up with my husband. Fortunately when I got back he had passed out on the sofa and I went safely to bed.

It seemed that in his alcohol-inflamed state he had also become unreasonably jealous, and I never dared to be alone or to talk too long to any of our male friends. On one occasion I needed to call into Thora's home with some query, so as Ron stayed in the car I ran and knocked on the door. Her husband Franz answered and invited me to step into the hall as Thora was through in the bedroom. I called out my query to her along the passage as Franz held the front door open and, having my answer, came out and back into the car. Ron drove off in a fury, pulled up at our house and fiercely accused me of kissing Franz in their hallway. I couldn't believe it – for heaven's sake, I had no interest in Franz and Thora was my friend, but his jealousy knew no bounds and no matter how careful I was he would find some way of accusing me of infidelity.

One day he told me with great glee that he had found out that there was a back entrance to the place where I worked and that he would be watching to see if I went out anywhere during my lunch hour. I realized I was dealing with a very disturbed man, and it showed up in his work, where although he could always get good jobs, before long he would have outstayed his welcome.

There seemed to be no end to our problems. Other people who had emigrated to South Africa at the same time as we had were able to make a good life for themselves, to buy a nice home, take care of and educate their children, but in my case, the inheritance I had been left by my father had been used up and nothing was being put in its place, despite the opportunities that abounded. And all the hard work that I did went to keeping us in food and clothing when it should have been the icing on the cake. But all of this was as nothing compared to the change in the man whom I still loved, and yet who was no longer the man I had met and married.

One night he came home late, long after Emily had washed up and returned to her room and Christopher was asleep in his bedroom. His speech was slurred, his clothes looked untidy and creased and as I berated him he turned his face up to me with his chin towards me and he said, 'Well, go on then! If that's how you feel, hit me! Go on, hit me!' As he swayed on his feet, all my fury and rage at the position he had put us into came to the surface, and without a second invitation, I drew back my arm, and with all my strength I hit him hard on the jaw. He staggered backwards, and before he could react, I turned and fled for the bedroom and locked the door. Before long, he had recovered enough to come and hammer on the door and shout at me to let him in, but I kept quiet and huddled on the bed. I heard him stumble away to the spare bedroom and listened as he struggled to undress. At one point it seemed that he had become entangled in his trousers as there was a loud crash as he fell on the floor. At last all was silent and I was left trembling and in tears during that dark night.

As I lay there I thought of all the things I had done to try and make him come to his senses, the pleadings, the quiet talks, the rows, followed by his hollow promises to stop drinking. The fiasco of the Alcoholics Anonymous meetings, even the fact of sending the children away, nothing seemed to have worked. And then I thought, there is one thing I haven't tried, I have never asked God for his help.

In the dark of that hot African night, I knelt by my bed and prayed for the help we so desperately needed. My prayer was simple and unconstructed, and almost as if He had been waiting for me to call, I suddenly felt surrounded by loving arms, bathed in warmth and compassion and I heard an inner voice say to me, 'Lo, I am with you always.' I crawled back into bed, comforted in a way I had never before known, and fell asleep.

The next morning when Ron came out of the spare room he had a large bruise on his face, whether from the blow I had given him or whether from falling against the frame of the bed, I do not know, but if he remembered much of the previous night, he made no mention of it and we got ready and left for work.

From that day on, however, things gradually changed. There was no overnight conversion but events arose which brought about fresh decisions, and the scene was eventually set for the answer to my prayer.

At that time we were both working in Johannesburg and travelling in every day, and so it was decided that we would move back into the city, or at least find a house in one of its suburbs. In addition, I wanted the children back again and I thought that a new start in a new place might be of benefit. So we moved to a suburb called Regents Park and rented a small house there. We had been living in Krugersdorp for over four years.

The little dog we had at that time became ill and Ron took him to the SPCA for treatment. Some time later he came back to tell us the sad news that he had died even as he laid him on the vet's table. The children were inconsolable and so we decided to get another dog to replace him. We all went to the kennels and walked slowly along the rows

160

of enclosures. There was no doubt about our choice, however, when we came to a cage with a large dog, a cross between a Rhodesian ridgeback and a mastiff sitting mournfully watching us. On enquiry we were told that he had been living on a farm where he had been ill-treated and was in great need of a loving family. We arranged for him to have all his injections and came back to collect him the next day. It was no easy task to fit him into our car, but with a bit of a struggle we got him in and took him home. He was pathetically pleased with all the attention he received, but we noticed that he didn't like his back to be touched, and we wondered if he had been beaten. We decided to call him Simba and he happily answered to that name.

One day, when the children and I had him out for a walk, a car backfired nearby and Simba went rigid and lost the use of his legs. We had a terrible struggle to get him home again having to almost carry him bodily, and again could only surmise that perhaps guns had been fired near him. But from then on he was the perfect pet and companion to us all. We loved him dearly and he returned our feelings to the hilt.

We soon discovered that the suburb we had moved to wasn't a very nice one so one weekend, we drove out to the northern suburbs of Johannesburg. We drove slowly around a recent 'extension', as new estates were termed, called Bryanston. The roads were largely still unmade and were pot-holed from the summer rains. As we drove carefully along we saw a house which was standing empty, so we stopped the car and went up the steep driveway to peer into the windows. It looked to be a good size, and around the back was a secluded terrace outside the lounge doors.

Across the road there was a rondavel (a round hut with a thatched roof) with a car parked alongside it and so we went over and knocked on the door, which was standing open. Inside was set up as an office and we asked the man inside if he knew anything about the house across the road. 'Everything,' he boomed. It seemed that he was in a position to rent it to us if we wished. He had the keys and so we went back up the drive and mounted the few steps to the entrance porch. The front door led directly into a large open-plan hall, lounge and dining room with the long lounge windows and double doors opening out onto the terrace that we had seen from outside. To the left at the back was the entrance to a big kitchen with cupboards reaching right up to the high ceiling. The back door opened out into a walled yard with a door on the left into the garage and another door into a laundry room. The lounge had a big fireplace at the far end and a door into a passage leading to the bedrooms, of which there were three, with built-in wardrobes in them all. The two smaller bedrooms faced into the back garden and the larger bedroom was at the front. We loved it and arranged to move in as soon as possible.

Once more this meant a change of schools for the children, but I had high hopes that this could become our permanent home and that Ron would benefit from being away from his pals at the Witpoortjie Hotel. As we moved in our next-door neighbour appeared at the door with a tea tray laden with cream scones and an enormous pot of tea. Hilda Hickenbothom was as gold hearted as they come, and she and her husband Len became firm friends. They had had their house built and Len had put in a swimming pool with changing rooms and a tennis court and our children were invited to meet their two children and to use the pool. Their son and daughter were a bit older than ours, but got on well. Hilda and Len had migrated from the Midlands and Len was an accountant, his rather dry manner counterbalancing Hilda's exuberance.

We decided to employ a house boy and gardener instead of a girl this time and Roger came to work for us. He was a gangly young man speaking very little English, but was hard working and pleasant. The children had acquired a chameleon as a pet and it was put to good use on the windowsills where its long tongue would shoot out and catch all the flies that found their way into the house. The manner in which it changed its colour intrigued the children to such an extent that I had to put a stop to their experiments with a range of colours before the poor thing died of exhaustion. When not catching flies on the windowsill it would happily rest on the dangling light fittings. Roger, however, was terrified of it and we had to banish it to its box whenever he came in to polish the floors. He also cleaned the windows, swept the terrace and weeded the garden. At the weekends I would do the washing on a Friday night out in the laundry at the back, leaving everything folded in a large tin bath ready to hang out the next morning. One Saturday I came out to find that all my washing, complete with the tin bath, had been stolen. This was unusual as there was very little crime in the area, but fortunately, for once, I had taken out house insurance and so was able to replace our sheets, towels and clothing with new stuff.

Truth to tell the garden was somewhat overgrown with rough grass at the front, and on the slope up from the terrace at the back, several large trees grew which the children loved to climb. One was a fir tree with very dense branches which Christopher climbed up one weekend. I was out in the garden when I heard a yelp, and then the top branches quivered and shook, then those a little lower down, then the next lot until bit by bit, Christopher fell the length of the tree and tumbled out at the bottom none the worse for his experience, apart from a few scratches. On another occasion I came home from work to find Paul with a plaster on his wrist. He had fallen out of the other tree while playing with our next-door neighbours' boy, and rather than disturb me, they had taken him to the local clinic and got him sorted out.

I loved our terrace and would happily sit there on warm summer evenings. We had bought a record player and one of the first records we bought was Nat King Cole with his beautiful selection of songs and I would sit out in the darkness as the words and melody of 'Star Dust' floated through the scented air.

Another favourite was a selection from *Aida* and I especially loved the final trio as the two lovers suffocate to death in their living tomb while the princess mourns above them.

When we had been living there for a few months, Hilda called me one day to say that they had made arrangements to visit the Kruger Park Game Reserve with some friends, but that unfortunately, the friends had had to bow out at the last moment. Would we like to go in their stead as everything was booked? It was rather short notice but too good an opportunity to miss. Apart from our trip to Durban, we had not seen a great deal of other parts of the country, so we managed to arrange for time off work and we set off early one morning for the Lowveldt and the Game Reserve. The park is about the size of Wales and in those days very undeveloped. It was quite a long drive, but at last we arrived at the main gates where we were checked in and from where we made our way along the unmade roads at the regulation slow speed of 20 miles per hour. It was forbidden to leave the cars at any time and we had to reach the campsite before sunset as the gates were closed then for the night. The camp was a large cleared area. The fence on the far side over which we could look was at the top of a slope leading down to the river, where crocodiles could be seen resting on the banks. Kudu and springbok were coming down for a last drink before sunset as we found our rondavel. These were circular traditional native huts made of mud and wattle and covered in white wash and with a high conical thatched roof. Inside they were immense, with a floor of beaten cow dung, tough and shiny, and with loads of space for our beds and simple tables and chairs. As nightfall approached, the native staff lit huge fires under the barbecues – or Braais, as they

164

were known locally – where the evening meal of meat and bread was served. After our meal we went happily to bed. Next morning we were awake early and stepped out into the crisp morning air. It was springtime and the jacaranda trees were spreading their lilac lace across the compound. Showers were simple; again, the native staff lit huge fires to heat tanks of water behind the shower blocks and we all happily showered and then ate a simple breakfast. The gates were opened again at sunrise and many enthusiasts had already left to try and spot lions at their early morning kill, the highlight of any visit. We set off a little later and before long were spotting many of the animals. The children were entranced and eagerly watched, trying to be the first to see something.

Ron had wound down the window on his side of the car as it was getting hot, when in the long grass in the distance we saw something coming bounding towards us. It turned out to be a troupe of baboons and the leader leaped up and tried to snatch Ron's glasses off. As he hastily tried to wind up the car window, in his panic he grabbed the wrong handle and his door began to open. Immediately the baboon grasped the car handle on the outside and attempted to wrestle it open. In the back the children were screaming and I was yelling at Ron to pull the door shut and move on. Eventually he did and we probably exceeded the 20 mph speed limit as we left the baboons behind.

We were only there for a few days, but on the second day Ron said he would have to drive out of the reserve for something or other. I cannot remember now what the excuse was, but with hindsight I realised he needed to buy some drink. Beers and spirits were not sold in the reserve and no doubt he was desperate for a drink. The children played contentedly at the campsite and I enjoyed the perfect peace as almost everyone had gone out for the day. Miles from civilization with no radios or telephones to disturb us, no traffic to be heard, only the silence of the African bush, the occasional snort of a hippo in the river or the scream of the monkeys, it was like going back to the beginning of time before mankind began to pollute the world.

The silence was shattered by a scream from Christopher, who had been happily standing with a banana in his hand, when it was suddenly snatched from him by a monkey which had leaped down from a nearby tree. Ron finally returned looking a lot happier with himself, but it was evident that he couldn't manage without his drink and I wondered if Hilda and Len were fooled by his excuse.

We had tried to take photos of the animals we saw but with our black-and-white films and small cameras, when we got home the results were disappointing. We did, however, have a few snaps of us all at the campsites standing outside our rondavel.

We didn't see a great deal of Ron's parents; the job at the Doonside holiday home had ended and they were back in Johannesburg. Every year towards the end of June I would get an urgent phone call from Margery, Ron's elder sister, with the message 'Not to forget Mother's birthday on July 3rd' and I would dutifully send off a birthday card. We never had a reminder for his father's but I always sent one anyhow. He was a wonderful man with a strong Lancashire accent and snow-white hair. Eventually they went as caretakers to an estate owned by the Prime Minister – I think it was Strydom at that time – and we went out to see them. It was quite a long drive south of the city beyond Vereeniging and they had a cottage in the extensive grounds. The main building was seldom occupied and their duties seemed to consist in monitoring the few staff kept on to look after the grounds. The area was mostly woodland with a neglected swimming pool but far too remote, we felt, for an elderly couple.

Tom and Iris were frequent visitors, however. Iris had had stomach problems for years and was being treated, not too successfully, by her GP. She became so ill that Tom finally put her in the car and took her to the Provincial Hospital in Johannesburg. In the casualty department they refused to see her without a doctor's letter but he would not be put off until, seeing how ill she was, they finally admitted her. They found that she was too weak for an immediate operation and had to build her up for several days before she had a partial gastrectomy.

Margery was a frequent visitor to the hospital. Her hypochondria was so severe that in order to get her off their backs, her GP of the moment would finally refer her for an operation. First of all it was a hysterectomy, and then a gall bladder removal; then it was an operation for haemorrhoids, then she developed lumps in her breasts. Ron joked that now they had taken out all they could from her intestines, she was growing lumps to keep them busy. No one in their right minds ever asked Margery how she was, as the ensuing description of her current medical condition could last for hours.

By and large, Ron's younger sister Miriam preferred to keep herself to herself although her husband, Ronnie Payton, was an outgoing and engaging fellow. There would be occasional family gatherings at places such as Giloolys Farm and at various swimming pools around the city. Ron was still drinking but it wasn't so severe – he seemed to be able to keep himself within bounds and I could cope with that. His jealousy was still there, however, and I had to take care when in mixed company not to seem to talk too long to other men, or to seem to be enjoying their company.

One of our favourite trips out was to Pretoria where we would take a picnic to the lovely grounds below the Union Buildings. Beyond the terraces of well-kept gardens was a swathe of sloping grassland with pine trees along the edges which provided shade on a hot summer's day. On one occasion as we sat resting after our meal, a little boy from an adjacent family came running past us calling out, 'Daddy! Daddy!' Young Christopher, then about three years old, leaped to his feet and shouted indignantly after him, 'It's not your Daddy! It's mine!' with all the passion his little soul could rouse.

Ron was working for an engineering firm selling large industrial-sized machines and also smaller tools for use on these machines. He seemed to be managing reasonably well and had been employed there for some time. The company selling the smaller tools was called Clarksons Tools and was based in England, everything being imported from the UK. They had decided, however, that they would set up their own sales base nearby and had leased premises and brought out one of their own managers to get it going. His name was Mr Worrall and he was looking for someone to do the clerical work. They were offering a good salary, so Ron mentioned my name and after an interview I got the job and resigned from the National Trading Company.

The offices were small and besides Mr Worrall and myself, they employed a store man, an Afrikaner called Ochie. We also had a young native boy to sweep the floors and make the tea. He was called Enos and unfortunately had an extremely ripe smell. He looked quite clean and no doubt washed well, but even so, to this day, I can recall that smell. The work was quite easy as we set up the office, installed telephones and Ochie, with the help of Enos, unpacked the tools and arranged them in their special shelving that had been installed in the next room. My job was to see to the invoicing and stock records, answer the phone, take orders and do the wages and any letters that needed typing. They used an accounting system called Kalamazoo which was quite ingenious, in that statements, invoices and stock records were all done at the same time – this in the days before computers, of course.

But without our realising it, trouble was brewing in the townships. Up until then we had not come across any trouble with the black population, crime was low in the white suburbs, we moved freely and without fear, and as we had no vote we were apolitical. We understood that the National Party of the Afrikaners maintained their majority by a manipulation of the voting boundaries. Cities such as Cape Town, Johannesburg, Durban and the rest only got to select one or two candidates, while the farming areas, while having a low population of Afrikaners, would send several MPs from each area, so that the opposition party, the United Party, only had a few seats. Helen Suzman was one such MP and made her presence felt in no uncertain terms, but she was vastly outnumbered. The pass system had been in place for several years and was strictly enforced to prevent too many blacks entering the cities, while jobs such as plumbing, bricklaying, or any of the trades, were reserved occupations for whites only. We heard very little in the newspapers of any trouble, although it was common knowledge that in the townships, crime was rampant. Bottle stores were not allowed to sell liquor to the blacks, but in the townships, the shebeens did a roaring trade making illicit liquor out of anything they could lay their hands on. The crime lords were known as 'tsotsis' and were reputed to use sharpened needles to push into the backs of their victims to paralyse them. The vast native hospital on the outskirts of town was called Baragwaneth Hospital and it was said that doctors from all around the world came to work there as a training ground as they were likely to see more trauma cases there over the course of a weekend than they would ever see in several years anywhere else.

Then, as we listened to the radio as we prepared for work one morning, we heard that there had been a terrible event at a township south of Johannesburg at a place called Sharpeville. The report said that the police station in the township had been charged by a black crowd and that the police had fought back and fired upon the crowd in self-defence. No other details were forthcoming but it seemed likely to us that a backlash might ensue and that there could possibly be an uprising among disaffected blacks against the white community.

Our two elder children attended school so would be quite safe, we felt, but I decided to take Christopher to work with me as a safeguard. Mr Whorral was somewhat astonished to see me arrive with my son, but put up no objection and Christopher spent the day happily drawing at a corner of my desk.

Overall, the business wasn't doing too well, and whether it was that or the incident at Sharpeville I never knew, but a few weeks later, young Mr Clarkson arrived from England with orders to close the business down. Ochie and I and the young native cleaner were given a month's wages in lieu of notice and I returned to the job agency once more.

The first job they found me was at an engineering firm on the outskirts of town. The owner of the firm was secretary of the Vaal Dam Yacht Club and he wanted the records sorted out for him. On my first day I was told I would work at a desk in his office, while the two women who did the office work for the firm were in the next room. They were not pleased with this arrangement and neither was I. The ladies' toilet was at the far end of the engineering works at the back of the building and I had to run a gauntlet of wolf whistles to get there. In addition, every time the owner had a business visitor, I was asked to leave the office and had to sit among the glowering clerks. I left at the end of the day and the next day went back to the agency and told them what I thought of the job in no uncertain terms. They were appalled, and phoned him in my hearing and tore him off a strip. So the next job they sent me to was a good one. The company was called United Dominions Corporation and they had large offices in a tree-lined square in the centre of town just opposite the Stock Exchange. The job was to do the statistics for the company, which financed loans for car sales companies across the country. I was given all the figures each month and had to calculate the percentages and prepare a report. At first I worked out the percentages manually, but then I was introduced to a machine, something like a pencil sharpener, which needed to be rotated backward and forward to produce the answer. No doubt, examples of such a machine can be found in museums somewhere nowadays, but it was a great help to me. The collated report then had to be typed and presented each month with an analysis for each region.

I enjoyed the work and found it quite within my capabilities; also, the salary was good and the people I worked with were great fun. One day, some of us decided to visit a fortune teller in town. A basement had been made into a sort of 'ghost train' scenario with spooky music and subdued lighting, and at the far end was the fortune teller. When it came to my turn and I had suitably crossed her palm with silver, she looked at my hand and said, 'You have four children.' 'No,' I said. But she insisted and said she could definitely see four children in my hand. We came out laughing, as things were so bad between Ron and I that I knew that there was no way I would ever have another child. He seemed to have lost all sense of worth and when he walked into the office to see me one day, I could hardly believe that this scruffy-looking man with alcohol on his breath was the man I had married.

12

Time had passed since I had had what I could only describe as a visitation by a higher power when I had called out for help that night in Krugersdorp. I felt somehow that things were moving but I could not see what the outcome of our situation was likely to be. My feeling was that there would come a time when we would have to separate somehow or other. Meanwhile the company for whom Ron worked were beginning to question his use to them as more often than not, his expenses claims did not match up with the amount of business he was bringing in and eventually he was asked to leave.

He decided he would set up a business of his own, the idea being that companies up and down the Reef who needed machine tools urgently would contact him and he would rush them to the firm and charge them for the service. He bought on credit a small green van which also had adequate seating for the family, rented an office and took on a young girl to answer the phone. Whether it could have worked or not we were never to find out as circumstances overtook us and the momentum of our affairs took an entirely different direction.

Iris decided to go to England with her daughter Karen to visit her family who came from Gloucestershire. She was one of a very large family with one son and several daughters. I had met one of her sisters, Hilda, who had also moved to South Africa and was living in Natal at a place called Pinetown. She had visited Iris once and kept us all enthralled with her tales of working in the Land Army during the war. Iris's brother, Arthur, sadly had died so she wanted to make

172

the trip to catch up with her parents and her sisters as they were a very close family. As she was to be away for some time, they gave up the lease on their house, stored their furniture in our garage and Tom came to live with us.

One Saturday morning, a few weeks after she had gone, I had to go into work to see to the end-of-month returns. Ron drove me in and as we were going along the Johannesburg streets, somehow a bee got into the car and it stung his hand as it rested it on the steering wheel. He cried out in pain and stopped the car and I managed to withdraw the sting. We carried on and he dropped me off at work. Later in the morning I received a phone call from Tom. It seemed that when he got back home Ron began to suffer from chest pains, so Tom immediately called our doctor who diagnosed coronary thrombosis and arranged for Ron to be admitted to hospital straight away. He was phoning me to tell me they were just about to leave the house. I went up to see my manager and explained the situation and was told to go and not to worry about the rest of the work I was doing. Bus services were a bit erratic so it was quicker to walk across town and up the hill to the Provincial Hospital, and by the time I arrived they were admitting Ron to the cardiac ward. I found him propped up in bed looking very pale and drawn and when I spoke to the doctor he said the worst seemed to be over and hopefully there would not be another attack. He would be kept resting in bed for the next few days until they saw that he had recovered. There was very little in the way of medication at that time and coronary thrombosis, where the arteries supplying the heart muscle became blocked by a blood clot, damaging the heart muscle itself, was not uncommon. After a few days they would do a cardiogram to establish how much damage had occurred.

Tom took me home and I phoned his parents and Margery who said they would visit him that night as I had the children to care for. On Sunday I took them to see their father. Visiting

173

was only allowed in the afternoons on Sundays, and apparently that morning when the doctor had just reached his bedside, Ron had had another heart attack from which he had been resuscitated due to the doctor being on the spot. He was very shaken so we did not stay long as I did not want to tire him. Visiting during the week was also restricted to an hour in the afternoon and then an evening visit from 7 p.m. for an hour.

So I began a routine of driving myself to work, where I finished at 5 p.m. and then would try to find a small café or somewhere I could sit and wait for 7 o'clock as it was too far to go home and come back again. Ron soon recovered his spirits and made friends with the other men on the ward. The man in the next bed was much the same age as Ron, and his wife and children came to visit at the same time as I did. When she found out that I had to fill in two hours before visiting, his wife insisted that occasionally I should come to their house and have a meal with her before going to the hospital. They were Jewish people and I found it quite fascinating to see how they ate, so different from what I was used to, and so tasty! Their kindness knew no bounds. Another couple came in every night to visit their son, a young man in his early twenties who was at university. He was a handsome young fellow but with a brick red complexion. Speaking to his parents as we would wait for the ward doors to be opened every evening, they told me that he had diseased kidneys and that nothing could be done for him. What strides medicine has taken since those days, and how frustrating for the doctors then that so little could be done. On one occasion, a doctor thought that it might help if Ron took a regular dose of linseed oil, and so he managed to swallow the terrible-tasting brew. When next the consultant did his rounds with all his students, he reached Ron's bed and asked him how he felt. With his typically ironic sense of humour, Ron replied, 'Like a well-oiled bat!'

Eventually, still pale and very shaken, he was allowed home. Meanwhile I had had to wind up the business and terminate the employment of the young woman taken on to answer the phones. Now, alas, we only had my income to rely on so once again I knew that we would have to find a cheaper home. I had loved the house at Bryanston and was sad to leave it, but had no choice. I found a house in Linden, a suburb north of Johannesburg. It was an older house and had been standing empty for some time. It was very basic but after giving it a good clean I managed to make it fairly presentable. It stood on a corner and had a long, unkempt garden at the end of which was a tumbledown building held up mainly by the creepers which covered it, but which became a favourite playground for the children. We had kept the little green van and I managed to continue the payments on it.

All of this, of course, could not have come at a worse time for the children. Anne was nine years old, Paul eight, and Christopher, at five years old, was soon to start school. It seemed that the tranquil family life I so much desired was once more beyond my reach, and the main ones to suffer were the children.

After his enforced period of sobriety, Ron was back to someone more like the man I had married, and I felt more confident of the future. We were tided over for a couple of months by a pay out from the government scheme which all workers had to pay into and then Ron went to look for some work that would not be too onerous.

Two things happened at around the same time. The first was when our little van needed a new tyre and I gave Ron the money to go and get one. The second was when the man who had employed him to work in a shop in the shopping mall phoned up to ask where he was. When Ron came home I knew he had been drinking again and when he handed me the bill for the new tyre I could see it had been altered.

Obviously he had not been able to resist the lure of getting some money, no matter how stretched we were financially, and had then made his way to the Witpoortjie Hotel with his 'latch lifter', sufficient money to buy his first drink in the hope that his 'friends' would stand him others.

I was stunned and the next day I rang in to say I would not be at work. Iris had returned from England and she was back at her old job where she kept the books for a night club called the Bal Taberin in central Johannesburg. I knew she was always on her own during the day, so I called her and arranged to go in. I took the invoice with me and from her office I phoned the company and asked them to look up what the cost of the new tyre had been. When they told me the charge, I knew that my suspicions were true and it was the last straw. After all we had been through, when he had been at death's door, when I had supported him and done all in my power to keep us going, he could still do this to us.

I told Iris that I would have to get a divorce before he took us all down with him, and so she phoned the solicitor who dealt with the club's affairs. He agreed to see me straight away and I walked the few blocks to his office. He listened to my story and then he told me that in South Africa there were only two grounds for divorce, adultery or desertion, neither of which applied to my situation, of course. I knew that Ron would never agree to a divorce because despite everything I knew he loved me and our children, but the solicitor suggested he send him a letter saying I wanted a divorce to see if we could force his hand. I went back to Iris and told her what the solicitor had said and then made my way home. When I got back, one of his pals from the Witpoortjie Hotel was there, a giant of a man, but with a good heart. He was castigating Ron in no uncertain terms and telling him that all his so-called friends at the hotel laughed behind his back because, when under the influence,

176

he tended to boast about all sorts of things he was supposed to have done. It seemed that they had recalled all his stories and added up the number of years it must have taken for him to have done all he claimed to have done, and on their reckoning he should by now be about 102! Ron was flabbergasted and had no reply; when this man left he dissolved into tears. But his rage was something to behold when a day or two later he received the letter from the solicitor saying I was divorcing him. He ranted and raved, swore he would employ the best solicitor in the country and he would have the children and I would never see them again! I feared for his heart at one point, so left the house while he cooled down. We had been married for ten years, and our children were leaving babyhood behind; the future looked very bleak.

The next few days were spent in an armed truce, neither of us speaking to the other, until on the Sunday he said he wanted to go to the Salvation Army service in the city. We drove there in silence and at the end of the service when, as in all Army services, the call is made for anyone who wishes to, to come to the Mercy Seat at the foot of the platform, to my surprise, Ron stood up, walked forward and knelt at the wooden bench.

We drove back to the house as silently as we had going there. Ron had been at the Mercy Seat for so long and so many people had prayed with him, that the majority of the congregation had left for home before he finally stood up and we left.

My feelings were in turmoil, I longed to believe that this was a genuine confession and call for help, but I could not help feeling that perhaps it was a ploy to prevent losing his marriage and his children. I had already made plans as to what my next move would be although I had not gone so far as to discuss it at work. I knew that as long as I stayed

177

in Johannesburg, Ron would seek me out and make our lives a misery. However, I knew I was well thought of at work and the company had a branch in Cape Town. I thought I would explain the situation and request a move to Cape Town and hopefully be able to find accommodation there and resettle with the children. Looking back on it, it was a desperate idea and may not even have succeeded, but in the event, it never came to that.

Ron found another job with the help of the Salvation Army and we began to attend every Sunday. He managed to stop drinking, although that took its toll as he must have had severe withdrawal symptoms. We began to talk again as time went by without him letting us down and I began to wonder if indeed a miracle had happened. Anyone who has had any dealings with alcoholism will be aware how rare it is for someone to be 'cured' overnight, but this seemed to be what had happened.

Eventually Ron told me what had happened. While he was in hospital and after the second heart attack, he said he prayed to God to forgive him and to give him five more years to, as he put it, 'redeem the years that the locust had eaten'. In other words, he had asked for the chance for a fresh start with the slate wiped clean. The Army were very supportive, but like me, they needed to know that this wasn't just a flash in the pan.

About this time Margery and Bram had acquired a holiday home on the South Coast at a place called St Michael's on Sea. Bram was an appeals officer for the Salvation Army and would be away from home all week travelling around various parts of the country and visiting donors to the work of the Army. One such man was an industrialist with a large factory just south of Durban and a large house in this popular holiday area about a two-hour drive south of Durban. Being a bluff, hearty man who was always 'hail fellow, well met' with all and sundry, Bram got on with him very well. The businessman and his wife had been at the races at Durban and his wife won a very large sum of money on a horse called 'C'est si Bon' and with her win she bought this holiday home for some reason, calling it after the horse. As they already had a large house in the area, Bram was asked if he would like to have the new purchase on very advantageous terms that he could repay by letting it out to visitors while still having the use of it himself during the school holidays. So the deal was set up, and when my holidays from United Dominions Corporation came up, Margery asked if I would like to go down with the family and, taking my sewing machine with me, make the curtains for the house.

So it was agreed and we went down for a very well-earned rest where Ron was soon recuperating from his illness. The house was on a lane running down to the sea so that every day the children could run down to the beach and along to the tidal pool nearby. I worked hard at doing the curtains but was able to have enough time to enjoy the break as well. Mother- and Father-in-law were acting as caretakers at the same businessman's house while he and his wife were on an extended holiday in Europe, so we saw quite a bit of them. I was very fond of my father-in-law with his white hair and Lancashire accent. He was a very handsome man right into his old age and always thought the best of everybody.

During those three weeks, Ron and I were able to spend time together again and gradually repair our relationship, so when he said that he would like to go back to being a Salvation Army officer once more, I gave it careful consideration. This of course was dependent on my being willing to become an officer in my own right, as both husband and wife must be fully trained in order to serve together. I gave it a lot of thought, but I had begun to see that this was the outcome of my cry for help so long ago. Christ had promised me that He would be with me always, and now this was the way that we were to go and I knew that I could trust His leading, so I agreed.

Needless to say, the Army was cautious and it was suggested that for the first year we would be appointed as Envoy and Mrs Malone, a noncommissioned officer and wife. We were to be appointed to the Linden Boys' Home as assistants to the new CO and his wife and during the year I would undertake a course of lessons to prepare me for entrance to the training college in September of the following year.

I sold our furniture as best I could; Ron's sister Miriam, when she heard we were selling up, told us she had always admired our dining-room suite so she bought that from us and a lady who said she had often admired our tapestry lounge suite through the windows of our lounge made us an offer for that. The remainder of our stuff went at knock-down prices, but I kept some of the china that had belonged to my mother. We moved to the boys' home, called Firlands, on Fourth Avenue, Linden in August of 1961, and fortunately, for once, the children could stay at the same school, where Christopher also now went. Simba of course went with us and was a huge success with the boys in the Home.

The Home was set on a large piece of land, a whole block, in fact, in this residential area. It was reached by a driveway with a small roundabout at the top, behind which were the main buildings which were all single storey. It was divided into two, with the older boys being in the charge of Tony and Ellen, the new COs, and with us caring for the younger lads from five to ten or eleven. Our section was a range of buildings set around as a quadrangle with the doors to the various rooms opening onto a broad, covered, highly polished red stoep set about four feet above the central area of short stubby grass. The entrance to the quadrangle was through a high archway and we had our quarters to the left as we went in. After our quarters, the first room on the left was a large airy one with a well-equipped medicine cabinet in it. Every

180

evening after supper and before bedtime, every boy who felt he had a problem would come and queue up at the room for attention. It soon became clear to me that most of their so-called cuts, bruises or whatever were largely imaginary and that what they really wanted was a bit of individual attention, so I never minded and would listen carefully to them all as it helped me to get to know them. Further round the square were dormitories with simple single iron bedsteads covered with colourful spreads and with a locker at each bedside. On the far side were the toilets and bathrooms where I bathed the smaller children myself each night, then at the front, a large room holding coats, sports gear, shoes and so on. The trick, I soon learned, of handling so many lively lads was to learn their names in double-quick time, so that any culprit could be readily identified.

Much as I loved the work, it meant that once more, my own children took a back seat while I attended to the needs of the boys in our care. There were very few orphans; mostly they were from broken homes and some of them were from large families with sisters in the Army's girls' home called Strathyre in Troyeville, Johannesburg.

There was a disused swimming pool which Ron repaired and had filled with water and all the children had great fun in that. Ron's job each day was to take those who needed it to the Children's Hospital, which would treat the boys as a GP would. Some would have to go to the dentist and there were always goods to be picked up somewhere.

One night Paul became quite ill with a high temperature and he was delirious, so we decided that Ron would take him with him to the hospital the next day. Anne spoke up then and told us that Christopher was regularly vomiting, something of which I was not aware. I knew that while we were in Bryanston he had had a few days when he had vomited now and again, but with no other symptoms I thought that it had passed. But it seemed that he had been quietly

181

going off by himself and had not told me. I was devastated, such a little boy and yet so stoic and I had not even noticed.

So next morning both Paul and Christopher went in the combi with their father and all the other boys requiring treatment that day. Paul was so ill that I expected that he might be admitted to hospital and that Christopher might be given some medicine to take and sent home. In the event, a shocked Ron arrived home with Paul while Christopher had been admitted. It seemed that they suspected he had a stomach ulcer and they were keeping him in for tests while Paul was diagnosed with tic bite fever and was given a course of medicine to take. It wasn't unusual for dogs and other animals to pick up tics on their fur which then burrowed into the skin and became fat and bloated on the blood they sucked from the animals. No doubt Simba had suffered from them and somehow Paul had been bitten as well, although we had not been aware of it. He was ill for some weeks and was a shadow of his former self before he began to recover.

After X-rays it was established that Christopher did indeed have a duodenal ulcer – at five, he was one of the youngest patients they had ever come across. When his teacher heard about it at school, she was in tears as she blamed herself for pushing him too hard. Later we were to discover that the poor child was dyslexic.

One problem still remained which would prevent us from fully entering the work of the Salvation Army, and that was the money we still owed on various debts we had incurred over the years. The solicitor in Krugersdorp wrote to us to say that he would no longer administer the monthly payments that we sent to him, and enclosed a list of all the companies he had been paying them to. Unfortunately he did not tell me how much each one was owed and refused to enter into any correspondence with me. So I phoned each one and arranged to make regular payments out of our small salary.

The only one that surprised me was the Necchi Company from whom I had bought my trusty sewing machine. They searched their records and said they could find no trace of an outstanding debt. That aside, I had no idea what we could do and how long it would take before we were free of this burden, but I should have known that God had a plan.

I had a letter from Auntie Ethel in which she said that she had had inquiries from Newcastle Corporation about a plot of land that my father and his brother had bought many years ago with the intention of building a garage for their trucks. After Stan died, Nancy had demanded her share of the business despite my father's pleas for her to accept an income and it had been a struggle for him to survive afterwards so the land had never been developed. It was listed as part of his estate that had been left to me, and now the corporation were making sweeping plans to develop that part of the city and were looking for the owners in order to buy the land.

I wrote back to Auntie Ethel and asked her if she would be prepared to act for me in the matter and she agreed. Before long the sale was concluded, the corporation paying £450 for the land at 16–22 Blagdon Street. After legal fees and a payment to Auntie Ethel of £15, I received a cheque for £426.9s.9d. at the end of November 1961. I phoned all the debtors and was able to send them a payment in settlement, and we were able to pay for our little van as well.

Tony and Ellen, who were in charge of the Home, were young for the command, but Ellen's father had run it prior to them and they had the added advantage of having been trained in England at the Salvation Army College on Denmark Hill in London. Ron himself had many happy memories of his training there in 1948, when most of the young men were recently released from their war service and took a somewhat irreverent outlook on themselves and life in general. He had a few old black-and-white snapshots of a group of

183

them in the grounds of the college and loved to reminisce about his time there.

However, the Army operated in 86 different countries at that time, and many of them now had their own training colleges, among which was South Africa. Therefore anyone trained in London, the hub of the Army's activities, had a certain caché, as it were. Ellen was a very large lady, reflecting her Afrikaner stock, and strode around with a self-satisfied air, while Tony was a handsome young man with a rugby player's build but very little to say for himself. Consequently, Ellen ruled their matrimonial roost and more often than not, we were left to carry on at the Home while she spent many hours at her parents' home or out shopping with her mother.

Most Army institutions had a trade card to use at one of the large wholesalers, and the Home was no exception. When we cleared our debts and had a bit of money, I went with Ellen to the wholesalers and was able to buy a good selection of clothing for the children. When the bill came in some weeks later I drew the money out of our bank and, as agreed that day, met Ellen at the Army Hall on Commissioner Street for the weekly Home League meeting which we both attended. I gave her the money and thought no more about it.

Christmas was a lively affair and we had a big party for the boys which the Mayor of Johannesburg and many other dignitaries attended. Afterwards there were presents for all the children, and mine received an inflatable boat, which was a huge success in the swimming pool.

More and more, however, we found ourselves being left in charge until the situation must have become known to Headquarters because suddenly in March of 1962 we were told we were to be transferred to the men's hostel on Simmonds Street in the heart of the industrial area of Johannesburg. My heart sank at yet another move, but we had no choice as I was to be entered into the training college later that year and it was explained to us that it would be easier for

184

Ron to manage his work and the family in that position, as he would be assistant again to an older couple, Brigadier Greenwood and his wife. His wife was a lovely lady, but he was a real pain and parsimonious to a fault. He had been appointed because the Home was in financial trouble and he was well known for his rigid budgeting. He used to give his wife and me a pound every week to take to the O.K. Bazaars which had recently opened up a new-fangled self-service grocery department, where Mrs Greenwood and I would take much pleasure in buying little extras for ourselves, biscuits and fruit for the children, perhaps some sweets and baking materials to use at home. Otherwise our food came from the kitchens and was the same as the men ate.

A few weeks later, the finance officer at Headquarters, a lovely fellow called Colonel MacDonald, took me to one side and asked me confidentially, and somewhat tentatively, about the goods I had bought while at Linden and whether I had paid for them. I told him exactly what had happened and that as I had given Ellen the cash at the meeting, I had not expected or received a receipt. At the time that we were moved, they had been transferred to the Eastern Cape and we heard little of them again, so I often suspected that somehow they had blotted their copybooks.

Of course this move meant another school for the children, but this was something the Army never took into account when they moved their people around. Usually, either one went into social institutions such as the many hostels run for the needy, or one went as a Corps officer, to run a Corps in the way that a minister of religion would run his church, but the Army theme was used from top to bottom. The General was the Leader of the movement and each country in which the Army operated was known as a Territory and was run by a Commissioner and under him was a Chief Secretary. Colonel Lewis was the Chief Secretary at that time and was well liked for his thoughtful manner and intelligence.

Headquarters was based in Johannesburg and the Territory was divided up into Divisions, each one under the command of a Divisional Commander or DC. There were four Divisions; the Transvaal (which is where we were), Natal, Eastern Cape centered at Port Elizabeth and the Cape at Cape Town.

At Headquarters there was the finance department, trade and the tailoring department, the DC for the region and the social secretary who had responsibility for the social institutions. These included, as well as the boys' home, three men's hostels, one in Johannesburg, one in Durban and one outside Cape Town called Muldersvlei. There was a girls' home and a women's refuge which was more for retired ladies than those with problems, and there was an unmarried mothers' home as well. In the centre of Johannesburg was a young women's hostel and on the other side of town, a young men's hostel. All these were aimed at white people, but outside the city was a training college for natives, and in Troyeville, a training college for whites.

Ron was still an Envoy, or noncommissioned officer, and I was due to enter the training college in September of that year. We had to buy our own uniforms, which were tailor made by the tailoring department at Trade, in Headquarters, where they also had a shop selling books, Bibles, commentaries and anything else a minister of religion might want. Our uniforms were navy blue serge in the winter with the traditional Army bonnet for me and cap for Ron, and in the summer I wore a cream uniform with a hat, while my working clothes were fawn belted overall, short sleeved in summer, long in winter, all having the requisite shoulder tabs designating rank.

Ron's job was to check the cleaners in the dormitories every day and fetch the groceries and fresh produce that had been ordered. At night he sat in the office checking in the men who came from the streets and taking their payments. They were given a good meal and used the showers and the next morning, after a cooked breakfast, they left for the day.

186

Sometimes fights would break out, but generally they were a good-natured lot and Ron enjoyed sitting with them in the gardens hearing their stories. Many had had homes and families and a recurring theme was the marriage break-up, the loss of jobs due to drinking and then the streets, where they would sit in the parks and beg when they were able. There was at least one ex-magistrate and one teacher among them and it made me realise how close we had come to the same fate for Ron.

And so began a period of great happiness, as at last, I had the husband and the family I had always wanted. It was wonderful to spend our days together and feel that we were working at something that God wanted us to do. Every morning after I had got the children up and given them their breakfasts, I would go to help Mrs Greenwood in the kitchens. We would supervise the kitchen staff as the breakfasts were served then see that everything was cleared away. The staff would then go and have their breakfasts while we entered the large room off the kitchens where all the stores were kept. This was always kept under lock and key as pilfering was an ever-present factor. Here we had industrial-sized refrigerators for the meat and dairy products and shelves stacked with catering-sized tinned goods. On raised platforms were sacks of flour, pulses and cereals, and near the door, large crates of eggs. One of the cleaners would go in with us, and as we checked on stocks and took out the goods necessary for the evening meal, he would clean the floor on his hands and knees with the special brushes used for polishing the shining red floors. Each week we would plan the menus and do the ordering and it was very good training for me.

In the afternoons I would do my studying or go to the library in town for reference books. The first modern translation of the Bible had just been produced, the New English Bible, and I read it as I would a novel. Suddenly the Bible story sprang to life as I traced the history of Abraham, Isaac and

Jacob and their descendants where previously I had only been aware of the small readings which accompanied a sermon. But it was the New Testament that grabbed my interest and I marvelled at the replies Jesus gave to those who would have baited him and tripped him up with questions on the Jewish Law. Every Sunday a service would be held in the residents' lounge, taken by either Ron or Brigadier Greenwood, but I always felt we did not do enough for the men. On several occasions Ron took a group of them to the evening service at the Salvation Army Corps on Commissioner Street, but they got some black looks from some of the regulars. Ron didn't care though and was immune to any criticism.

Winter that year was very cold. As we were 6,000 feet above sea level, frosts at night were quite usual, but as there was no rain for three months, everything became very dry. But one morning we woke up to find that there had been a fall of snow, something that had not been known to happen as long as anyone could remember. The children were enchanted and in the garden at the back of the old building, they ran around making snowballs, while Simba, wild with excitement, leapt into the air attempting to catch them.

Soon it was time for me to prepare to enter the training college on 3 September, strangely enough on Ron's birthday. I would be living there full time and had to take leave of the children as no allowances were made for anyone with a family, but I knew that we were lucky to have been accepted considering Ron's past. However, I was determined to make the most of the opportunity and made my farewells with as cheerful a countenance as I could.

13

The training college was situated in Troyeville on a hill overlooking Bezuidenhout (or Bez) Valley just off Appolonia Street. It was a large late Victorian building with several outer buildings, called Clarence House, possibly after the gold-mining magnate who had originally built it. The main entrance was approached by a steep set of stairs and the entrance hall was spacious with a curving staircase off to the right. On the left at the front was a large sitting room, the private quarters of Brigadier and Mrs Von Kleist, while on the right was a large room, the brigadier's study. Behind the staircase on the right were the kitchens and pantry, and on the left was a dining room and beyond that a small sitting room for the use of the cadets.

Upstairs, a room had been partitioned off for the women cadets, among them, Maureen Miller, whose husband was already a lieutenant in charge of the Corps in Krugersdorp. Then there was Josephine Graham, a young girl from the Eastern Cape, Hilary Browski from Johannesburg and myself. I think there was another girl but my memory fails me as to her identity. Our room looked out onto the garden with a small fish pond and beyond that was a recently built chapel. To the left was the main lecture hall then through a gate into a yard where the men's quarters were on the left and on the other side of the yard was a two-storey building with a bathroom and laundry below and a range of rooms above, sometimes used for visiting guests.

Until now, the period of training had been one year, but it had just been extended to two. Each training session was given a name which was used by all the training sessions in all the colleges around the world. Ours was to be 'The Heroes of the Faith'.

As I settled in it seemed strange to be no longer among the noise and turmoil of a young family, but the college routine was soon established and although I missed my family, it was good to have time for myself and to concentrate all my efforts on my studies. I had spent much time preparing for this change and had made many outfits for Anne to see her through until I could sew for her again, but I had reckoned without her sudden spring into puberty and before long, none of her new clothes fitted her. Other than that arrangements went fairly smoothly, although before long I discovered that Brigadier Greenwood had withdrawn the £1 a week for a few treats for my children. I took the chance of mentioning this to the social secretary, Hesketh King, next time I saw him, and Mrs Greenwood was given the extra £1 to buy the things she knew I usually got for them. I felt I was making sacrifice enough without the children having to suffer as well.

Our classes were held in the lecture hall sitting at school desks. We learnt Doctrine, Bible Study, Orders and Regulations and Salvation Army Methods and Procedures, which involved sermon construction and open-air work.

We had a Welcome Meeting at the Fairview Corps Hall, a massive building, which was packed for the occasion as the new intake of cadets was always of interest. I was chosen to speak on behalf of the women cadets and had my first experience of standing up before a large congregation. I spoke of the Army's historic placing of women at the forefront of the work on equal terms with the men, at a time when women had few rights. Catherine Booth, the wife of William Booth, the founder, was a woman of firm beliefs and I have no doubt that she it was who saw to, and also realised, the important work that women were capable of.

We attended the Holiness meeting at the Central Corps on

190

the Thursday evening, and after the service I was told that I could go home with my husband and to be back at 9 a.m. the next morning when we would all be allocated our household duties. It was good to be back at home and to be able to see the children off to school the next morning. Fridays were busy days at the college as all the cleaning was done by the cadets in the morning and in the afternoon we did our studying.

I soon settled into the routine of college life and enjoyed the challenge of the lectures. I found that my reading of the Bible paid off and was surprised to find that my fellow cadets, who in some cases had spent many years in Sunday School as well as adult meetings, were quite startled that I knew the sequence of events in Bible history; I had thought that I would be the one to lag behind and I have no way of accounting for this. We had a captain, Captain Hines, who came in on a daily basis to take some of the lectures. He was a talented pianist and accompanist and he soon had us organised into an effective choir. I was glad to use my voice in a more structured manner although there had always been much pleasure to be had in the singing we did at home, where Ron's lovely tenor voice blended so well with mine.

We were to be sent off for a week to experience some of the social work of the Army, and while it might have seemed reasonable to send me to be with my family at the men's home, it was decided that I would go to Doonside, near Durban, where the erstwhile holiday home had been turned into a retirement home for elderly ladies. I caught the train from Johannesburg and on arrival in Durban was met by the Corps officer, Captain Stephenson, who drove me along the coast to Doonside. The building was much as I remembered it from our holiday a few years previously but it was now being run by a lady who, in appearance, was much of an age with her residents. Her energy, however, was astounding, and she could run me off my feet any day of the week. She

191

set me to a list of tasks which she had obviously been saving up just for me and kept the best for last. She took me to a room off the main kitchens which, when opened, was found to contain bundles of wrapping paper, balls of string and cardboard boxes which she must have been hoarding for some years. My task was to sort it all out and put it in some sort of order. After I had spent a couple of days in there during the odd hours when I was not otherwise serving meals, sorting laundry or helping in the kitchens, she took pity on me and gave me a few hours off. I gladly escaped down to the beach and spent a few precious hours just sitting and watching the sea.

A few weeks after our return from social work experience, we began our preparations for our campaign. Each session went on campaign to a different part of the country for a period of meetings and rallies and we were to go to the Eastern Cape. We travelled in the college's combi and took most of one day to drive down to East London in the Eastern Cape Province. We were billeted with various families and Maureen Miller was able to go and stay with her family – they lived in a modest little house which seemed to be overflowing with small children.

From East London we went to Port Elizabeth, where Josephine came from. Her family lived in a prefabricated series of buildings on the edge of a disused airfield. They obviously had few of this world's goods, but were warm and welcoming. A young captain had gone there to start a Sunday School some years before and had been so successful that as well as Josephine going to college, her younger sister was to follow her later.

From there we travelled to Kimberley where, as well as attending and taking part in meetings, we were taken to see the diamond mines.

When diamonds were discovered in the 1800s, the early prospectors each staked their small claim and proceeded to dig downwards. Some claims went down faster than others; they went deeper and deeper, complicated pulley systems were needed to haul up the clay and an enormous hole going down many hundreds of feet was the final result. Standing on one side of the hole, the town of Kimberley on the other side of it looked like a range of doll-size buildings, so vast was the circumference. Alongside, some of the original corrugated iron dwellings had been preserved with a wonderful range of old photos showing the people of that time. We were also taken to the modern day mine, where, as with the gold mines, Africans from many parts of the continent came to work for set periods of time. As IDB (illegal diamond buying) was a scourge of the industry, the mine workings were fenced around and everything that the men could want was provided on the site. There were football fields (the preferred game of the Africans), sports centres and churches. One we went to see was built to resemble a wigwam and inside, its circular seating and beautiful windows were quite striking. At the entrance to the living blocks, there were noticeboards with photos of grinning black men with narratives beneath telling who they were and what their reward had been. For if, while working, a large diamond might be found among all the clay being dug out, then if it was handed over, the finder got a large reward and was sent back home with money aplenty to buy himself cattle and a wife ... or two. Thus they were encouraged not to barter with the IDB industry.

We were taken round the works where the huge rollers crushed the ore to smaller pieces which were then passed through further rollers covered with a Vaseline-like substance, which caught up the diamonds. We were shown, behind protective glass, the previous day's takings of diamonds. It seemed a very small amount for such an enormous under-taking.

Back at the college we began to look forward to the end of our first year and to wonder what would be in store for us. Apparently we would no longer be at the college on a full-time basis, but would be given responsibilities in the field, either as assistants at local Corps for those who would undertake further training to be Corps officers or, in my case, to a social work centre. June of 1963 was approaching, when all this would be decided.

Throughout our marriage, whenever we were apart for any length of time, Ron and I would exchange letters, and my time at the training college was no exception. He would write to me in the evenings when he would be on duty at the hostel's office and tell me of the day's doings and of the children's welfare. One letter contains a poem that he wrote at the end of such a letter, saying, 'In conclusion, silly jingle!!—

The Portals locked, the men abed, I sit and rest my
    great big head,
Tumultuous thoughts of busy day, bidding the waiting
    Orpheus stay,
Simba sleeps with head on paws, dreams of food and
    moves his jaws.
Gone the patter of 'tiny feet', three little angels fast
    asleep,
Preparing for the coming morn (with raucous cries
    they'll greet the dawn!!)
The blessed cool of evening spreads; gentle stirring
    in small beds.
Today God has been good to us, in work and play, in
    peace and fuss.

Then through the calm of balmy eve, the sound of
    distant thunder.
A thought occurs:- "Whom God hath joined—
LET NO MAN PUT ATUESDAY"

      Milton (Malone)

Don't bother, I'll pull the chain!!'

Eventually the news came: Ron and I were to be appointed in charge of the Young Men's Hostel, Park House, in De Korte Street in Braamfontein, and two months later we were promoted to the rank of lieutenant. We soon settled in to the work there, where young men from a variety of backgrounds were housed in single rooms in a safe and pleasant environment. We had our private rooms at the front of the house with a light and spacious living room on one side of the passage and a series of smaller rooms on the other side. At the rear were the large kitchens where the cook, Jack, reigned supreme. He was of some indeterminate mixed race and we got on well. I always consulted him when planning the menus and his team of kitchen helpers worked efficiently and well.

We were due a holiday and planned to go to Durban for three weeks. The arrangement was that we had to find a replacement for us among the retired officers, and there was always a great demand for their services. We managed to secure Major De Villiers, as our stand in and the deal was that he only really acted as caretaker and I had to ensure that all the menus were planned and the orders placed for the groceries and so on, as well as seeing to all the finances before we left. It was a hectic time and perhaps we became a little careless, because as we sat on the beach at Durban I sent the children off to buy ice creams, and as the three of them walked away, in my mind's eye, I could see a fourth little figure alongside. The news of another pregnancy was not, initially, a welcome one, really, for either of us, but before long the idea of having another child born into our now stable and loving family was an attractive one. Additionally, it now became clear that the fortune teller, so many years ago, had been correct, I was to have four children. When we told the children they were delighted. Christopher said, 'Oh good! I won't be the youngest any more!' And Anne exclaimed, 'Oh! I have been praying for this to happen!' Our holiday was wonderful and a great time to be together

195

again and I have a lovely photo of Ron with our children on the deck of one of the Union Castle ships which happened to be in dock at that time.

During the preceding years I had taken very little interest in political or international events. While I had been working at the National Trading Company, I had, along with the others in our office, tuned in to Macmillan's 'Wind of Change' speech and since then, successive African nations had been given independence from their European masters. In 1960, in the Belgian Congo, the initial handover appeared to go well, but then descended into terrible anarchy and chaos as Patrice Lumumba faced threats from Moise Tshombe in Katanga province. UN troops were sent in and found themselves facing paid mercenaries and the resulting toll of dead and maimed would probably never be fully known. Later, the Mau Mau in Kenya began their horrific programme against white settlers and Jomo Kenyatta's name became a byword for terror and slaughter. Many missionaries were caught up in that and fled, some of them to us in South Africa.

Since Sharpeville, it seemed that the Afrikaner authorities had become more strict in their relations with the black population, but for all of the white population there was a feeling of unease about our safety. At that time, there was, in addition, suspicion about the agenda of Russia and the communist threat. While there is little doubt that Russia at that time harboured the idea of infiltrating parts of Africa, this was a useful tool for the Afrikaner government, as the Rivonia trials proved. Several men were arrested, including Nelson Mandela, after it was claimed that they had sophisticated radio equipment at their isolated farmhouse. Communists were seen behind every bush, if not under every bed.

Historically the situation in South Africa was a complicated one. The country was first discovered by Portuguese sailors in the 1600s and later, the Dutch East India Company set

196

up a small colony in the Cape where vegetable gardens produced fresh fruit and vegetables for the sailing ships on their way to and from the Dutch East Indies. They carried the lucrative spices to Europe and after it had been discovered that the dreaded disease of scurvy among the seamen could be prevented by a better diet than the hard biscuits they had previously survived on, it proved essential to stop over and restock with fresh produce. The colony had grown, the original Bushmen either perished or moved away, and the gardens were serviced by Malays brought from the East Indies for the purpose.

Holland eventually sold the Cape Colony to the British who, in the wake of the passing of the anti-slave laws presented to Parliament by William Wilberforce in 1789 and passed in 1807, demanded that the Dutch settlers, or Boers (meaning farmers), should free their slaves. In protest they left their land and took themselves, their cattle and their people off into the hinterland of this vast country in a series of swarms called the Great Trek.

For the Afrikaners, this was the basis and grounding of their culture in which they took great pride. Hence the Voortrekker Monument outside Pretoria. Finally, up on the Highveldt they found vast unpopulated areas where only the occasional roving band of black people might be found and there they established their seat of government in Pretoria under President Kruger. All might have developed in a different way except that, twenty miles away from his capital, gold was discovered and before long, prospectors from around the world were swarming across the veldt and setting up camp, which became known as Johannesburg.

Meanwhile, diamonds were discovered at Kimberley and yet more prospectors flooded in. President Kruger was furious and as Johannesburg became larger and began to demand a say in its government, trouble soon escalated as Kruger refused any rights to these 'uitlanders'. The Boer War, as mentioned before, still left a sour taste in the mouths of the authorities at this time and generally speaking, the English-speaking population had no vote, or if they did, it counted for nothing because of the way the voting constituencies were arranged.

As well as English and Afrikaans people, there were also many Portuguese who had fled from Mozambique following independence. Then there were Chinese who had been brought in at one time to work in the gold mines, while in Natal, there was a large Indian population who, many years before had been brought in to work in the sugar plantations as indented labour and who, if they wished, would be repatriated back to India once their term of service was over. Most opted to stay, and although they suffered from the same curtailments as the black people, they nevertheless managed to run successful businesses and were a wealthy and well-structured part of the population.

So this was a complicated situation and sometimes it felt that we sat on a time bomb and that one day there would, without doubt, be some sort of a blood bath. Meanwhile we led our lives, hoped for the best and kept our passports up to date.

Generally speaking, blacks and whites lived parallel lives as obviously we had no black neighbours, even though most of us had a maid or gardener living at the back of our homes. I always found those with whom I was in contact to be cheerful and willing and I never needed to be harsh or unpleasant. It was understood, of course, that anything that wasn't nailed down would in all probability disappear, but one lived with that and took the necessary precautions. Everyone thronged the city and stores and rubbed shoulders in the streets, but come nightfall, the streets cleared and the loaded trains took the black people back to their homes in the townships.

The Afrikaners were somewhat humourless and dour, while

the English among us clung to our sense of humour. One day Ron and I went to see a matinee of one of the early *Carry On* films. It was *Carry On Nurse* and we were among the few in the cinema who hooted with laughter when the wife of the snooty patient produced a new dressing gown and said, 'I got it with my divi from the Co-op.'

My pregnancy went well, I attended the ante-natal clinic at the maternity hospital up the road and at the same time, I spent three days a week at the training college, as well as running the hostel. Ron was quite unable to handle the finances and it fell on me to see to those as well as run the kitchens, but he supervised the cleaners and spent time with the residents. He had also started writing articles and poetry for the *War Cry*, the Army's weekly paper which was produced in Cape Town. One of his poems was entitled 'Our Hoboes' and the only line I remember was, 'Each park bench, a poor man's throne'. In addition, he was a very talented public speaker and he would often be called upon to take services. He had the ability to write down three headings on the back of an envelope and then preach a riveting sermon around them.

Cathleen was born about 6 p.m. on 24 April 1964. Fathers were not allowed to be with their wives in those days, but Ron came and saw us straight afterwards and then he went home to tell the children they had a new little sister. When I went for my post-natal check, the doctors were not too happy with the state of my cervix and I was sent to see the gynaecologist. After examining me he explained that there was some breaking down of the tissue and that, although I was rather young for such an operation, he thought that a hysterectomy might be in order. He suggested that I should go home and talk it over with my husband. I rushed home, burst into the house and said to Ron, 'Guess what!' with great delight. This of course in the days just before the advent of the Pill.

Some weeks later I entered the general hospital for my operation and my sister-in-law Iris cared for Cathleen while I was in. I needed someone to work for me who would be able to help me with Cathleen as I had so many other duties, and in the time-honoured fashion, I asked the ward cleaner if she knew of anyone. The next day she said her friend was looking for work so I told her where to come and see me once I was home again. And so Toni came to work for us. Her full name was Antonia but she preferred to be called Toni. She had a home in the township to which she travelled every night and where she lived with her daughter Veronica. Her husband had deserted her some time previously. She was barely 5 feet tall and almost as round as she was high, with a few teeth missing at the front, but her personality shone through and we took to each other from day one.

Our session of cadets was due to be commissioned six weeks later and at our Dedication Service, Cathleen was dedicated to God as well. I could not have been more happy. After all that we had gone through, God had brought us safely through with our family intact and with a worthwhile future for us all.

When Cathleen was four months old we were due another holiday and we managed to arrange to have the use of a cottage in the grounds of the Army's Conference Centre in the Magaliesberg Hills to the west of Johannesburg. It was reached by secondary road off the beaten track on a gentle slope overlooking the hills. As it was winter, the air was crisp and clear and the smell of the eucalyptus trees was all-pervasive.

The main buildings were rather old and dilapidated but were not in use at that time, so we settled in to the cottage in the peace and remoteness of the area. The boys brought their roller skates and enjoyed skating around the patio, Cathleen rolled and kicked on a blanket under the grove of pine trees surrounding the cottage and we were able to use the swimming pool. Such a wonderful, restful holiday where we could recharge our batteries. The thought of those few days brings tears to my eyes today. How fortunate we are that we may not see what the future holds for us.

This was also a time when I was able to pay more attention to the needs of my children. Anne had had her eyes tested at school and I was told she was in need of glasses as she was short-sighted. All was arranged and as we left the shop with her new specs she pointed to an enormous advertising billboard and exclaimed that now she could see it! Obviously she had had a bigger problem than we had realised, but getting her to wear her glasses was another matter. Paul had also developed a problem with his eyesight when it became apparent that he had a lazy eye. He had worn glasses for some time, but on a regular check-up it was decided that the lenses were no longer strong enough to correct the eye. So he was admitted to hospital for an operation to correct it surgically, which was completely successful.

Following on his diagnosis of a duodenal ulcer, Christopher had had no further problems, but his ears tended to stick out from his head. This was causing some teasing at school and so I took him to the Children's Hospital and asked for an operation to correct the problem. Considering his medical history, they agreed to do it and so the flap behind his ear was cut and the muscles released so that his ears were set against his head. I have often wondered why the Queen did not have a similar operation done on Prince Charles when he was young!

Fortunately, apart from the hysterectomy, my health was good, but I discovered that I could obtain dental treatment at the dental hospital not far from us in Braamfontein. It was attached to the University of the Witwatersrand and trained the dental students. At each visit they would undertake a part of the treatment, which would be checked by the professor, and one would have to go back the following week to continue. A time-consuming process, but as I lived nearby I could pop in quite easily during the morning when duties were lighter. Thus I had crowns done on my front teeth, gold fillings in the back and complicated bridgework that we could never have afforded otherwise.

Medical treatment was good and the cost depended on income, and as we did not receive a large salary we were eligible for practically free treatment for ourselves and for the children.

About that time we exchanged our car for a camper van. It had been customized by the previous owner and had a fine selection of cupboards, two facing seats with a table between and a two burner cooker and a small sink. We also bought a tent to attach to the side and took it out for a trial run to a place on the Vaal River bank. On the way there, Paul, who had been eating an apple while sitting in the back with me and the other children, decided to throw out the apple core, leant forward, and before I could stop him, opened the door to dispose of it. I was able to lean forward to grab him and just managed to hook my fingers into the pocket on the back of his shorts, while shouting to Ron to stop the car. For some minutes I held on as the tarmac of the road swept by within inches of Paul's face, until we slowed down and stopped and I could drag him back in. Another close call for my son!

As 1964 drew to a close, we knew that there would be changes, as officers were moved around on a regular basis. Ron's health was reasonably good but from time to time he suffered from attacks of angina and sometimes he went into hospital for a day or two. So we confidently expected that we would be given an appointment that was not too heavy. We knew that the Durban Men's Home was smaller than the Johannesburg one and this seemed a distinct possibility to us. So we were somewhat dismayed to be told that we would be going back to Simmonds Street in charge but without an assistant. On 21 December we were both promoted to captain and on 14 January 1965 we moved back to Simmonds Street.

We could have had the more modern quarters at the top of the new building at the rear of the property, but as we did not have an assistant it was necessary to be at the front where we were nearer the entrance and the kitchens. We were fortunate that one of the men had been trained up to look after the office at night and another was able to do the books, so I was relieved of that duty. I soon got the kitchens and the menus sorted and had the storeroom spick and span. But I couldn't understand why eggs kept disappearing from the large wooden boxes on the floor near the door, until one day I happened to look around and saw Simba, who always followed me wherever I went, quietly put his head in the box, extract an egg and lope off with it. The thief was found!

We provided a cooked breakfast for the men who ate in the large dining room at the front of the building, a lunch of sandwiches and coffee for the older, retired residents at the back where they had their lounge, and at night a hot meal for all those who came to find a bed each night. It was not unusual to be woken up at night by someone from the hospital asking if they could send a vagrant to us, but we had to tell them that all our beds were taken every night as soon as the gates were opened. Of course, had we been able to accept any more, the hospital would have had a steady stream of candidates looking for an easy way to get in.

The work was not for the faint hearted as these men had no resources and had reached the bottom of the pile, but we did what we could, although the Joburg Corps were not too keen on a group of smelly hoboes cluttering up the back seats during the Sunday evening Salvation meeting, but Ron didn't care. As he said, that was what the Army was for. In any event, he held a service for the residents every Sunday which was very well attended.

203

This was the centenary year for the Salvation Army and the current general, General Coutts, was visiting many of the eighty-six countries in which the Army operated at that time. He came to South Africa early in the year and there were a series of well-attended meetings on the Transvaal. After a short visit to other places, it was planned that he would visit Cape Town before returning to the UK. We were due our annual leave and so we packed up the combi and set off for Cape Town in order to take in the final celebrations in a city we had not seen since our arrival in the country over ten years before. As usual we made a start in the early hours of the morning with the beds set down in the back where the children could sleep if they wished, while at the very back, above the rear engine, Cathleen was tucked in on her cot mattress which fitted in exactly. Sitting together at the front, Ron and I were able to relax and enjoy the passing scenery. The plan had been to stop somewhere en route, but the driving went so well that Ron decided, after a short rest, to push on and do the 1,000-mile trip in one go. At last we drove up the last line of hills and beyond, laid out below us, was Cape Town set around the sweep of the bay. We were to stay with friends, Captain and Mrs Hall, who were stationed in Cape Town and with whom Ron had been at college. They had two older children about the ages of our eldest, and one of about four years old nicknamed Nomi for some reason, a child to be avoided at all costs. For ever after her name would be mentioned with dread by my own family.

We were happy to be welcomed into their chaotic home, however, and squeezed into the available space, with some of us sleeping outside in the camper van. A big rally was to be held at Muldersvlei, the men's home based on the outskirts of the town, and we set off in good time to get there. However, we fell foul of the brand new motorway system and found ourselves, willy-nilly, being taken off

204

towards the airport. At last we found a place to turn back and managed to arrive just in time. On the journey, however, as we drove along, I found what felt like some sort of advertisement being played through my mind, and as I tried to grope for the memory, I suddenly felt as though I was going to faint. It was the oddest sensation and I found it difficult to explain to Ron what it had felt like. Anyhow, all seemed to be well again and we had an enjoyable day. We spent another day in Cape Town visiting the fish quays where Ron was photographed holding several fish as though he had caught them himself. We took our cine camera and filmed Cathleen in her little pink dress coming to terms with the sand on the beach.

We left Cape Town and travelled up the Garden Route along the coast, camping at Port Elizabeth and East London before travelling through the Transkei. At one point our vehicle had to be ferried across a river on a pontoon which was held by chains and physically pulled across by a team of black workers, chanting as they toiled. At last we reached the camp site at St Michaels on Sea where Bram and Margery, were staying at their cottage with Mim and Ronnie and Mam and Dad. We spent a few days there with them before setting off back up to the Transvaal. It had been a wonderful holiday and we had seen more of the country than ever before.

Back in Johannesburg, we settled once more into our routine. One day the police came to ask if we had taken in any suspicious characters. There had been a horrendous discovery of several body parts in a lake near one of the mines to the west of the town and they came complete with colour photos of the pieces. After giving them tea and biscuits, it became evident that they were in no hurry to leave despite the fact that there was little we could tell them, and so at last I had to gently suggest that they take their investigations elsewhere. They took it in good part and departed, but I don't think they ever found out either who the victim was or who had done the killing and the cutting up. On another occasion I was asked to attend to one of the men in the dormitories, so, sending one of the cleaners in first to announce that Matron was coming in, I examined the man in the bed who was complaining of pain in his chest. When I drew back the bedclothes I found that he had a very neat stab wound on the left side under his heart. An ambulance was called and he was taken to hospital, but he either did not know or could not recall who had stabbed him.

We had one death – again, I was called to the dormitories, where an older man had obviously died of natural causes during the night. We called the undertakers who normally saw to funerals paid for by the authorities and Ron went down to see them to make the necessary arrangements. At the funeral he took a group of the men with him, so that the poor fellow had a few people to sing some hymns for him. Ron told me he had bartered on the price with the funeral directors in that jokey manner of his and when shown the designated coffin had insisted it was a second-hand one because he could see the marks the screwdriver had made when it had been used on a previous occasion.

The man we had on the desk at night was a reformed alcoholic and we were glad of the work he did as we were working without an assistant, but one day we had a phone call from the social secretary, Colonel Hesketh King, asking Ron to go into Headquarters to see him. Ron came back absolutely fuming. Apparently there was a crisis at Muldersvlei in the Cape and they were desperate for some help. It had been decided that the man working in our office would be the ideal person to travel down and take over running their office. Although he fought against it with all his might, Ron was overruled, and so this man was put on the train for Cape Town with some money for his expenses. Of course, what Ron had warned against happened; when he was met at Cape Town he had spent all the expenses on drink, boasting to all and sundry that he was off to work for the Salvation Army, and so a good man was lost to us, to the people in the Cape, and worst of all to himself. Such were the cockeyed solutions that those in charge of us came up with, and before the year was out, although I did not know it, I was to be the victim of one of their worst miscarriages of organisation.

Cathleen was developing well and happily crawled around the flat. I had a little room for her in which was a cream-painted cupboard where I stored her clothes in the drawers above and her nappies in the cupboard below. We had a little cat at that time which loved to hide away in small spaces and it was quite usual to open one of the drawers to find the cat pop up, having climbed up through the spaces at the back. I usually changed Cathleen on the bed there and would drop the wet nappy onto the lino floor while I sponged her and put the new one on. One day I was interrupted by a knock at the front door, and after I had seen to the caller, I came back into the room to find the nappy had disappeared. As Cathleen and I were the only ones in the flat and as she couldn't tell me what had happened, it remained a mystery until I needed to get out the next dry nappy, where I found that she had carefully put the wet one away with the others. Just on a year old and already showing her lifelong passion for neatness.

Christopher had been having problems with reading and writing at school, and his teacher at that time, a young man, asked to see us. He said he thought he was suffering from dyslexia, a term we had not come across before. He explained it as being a sort of word blindness which had only recently been discovered and this was the first case he had come across. He offered to come to our home and to give Christopher remedial lessons to try to help him to deal with it, and so it was arranged. Poor child, first his stomach ulcer, then his ear operation, and now this. However, we were very grateful that it had been detected and that there was something that could be done about it. I did not entirely understand what the process was but it seemed to involve covering over some of the printing in some way. We only hoped it would prove to be successful.

Summer was coming to an end and as winter approached, Ron had several bouts of angina which meant he had an occasional hospital stay. He found it very upsetting in those large public wards when someone died more or less in full view of the rest of the ward. He was also feeling very tired from time to time, so I got into the habit of taking the children out on a Saturday, our day off, in order to give him some time to rest. We visited the museum on the floor above the library, the Stock Exchange and the fire station, where they were allowed to climb all over the huge machines. The favourite by far, however, was a secluded river bank I had discovered just outside Johannesburg. A low concrete bridge crossed the small stream down in a shallow valley, and just before the bridge was a dirt slip road which, if carefully manoeuvred, gave access to a quiet spot. Here we would park the combi and I would lay out rugs. We could take Cathleen's pram which doubled as a carrycot and Simba went too. Here the children played happily all afternoon, jumping across the streams on the rocks and sailing pieces of wood down the gentle flow. Bilhazia was a deadly disease caused by a snail in the water, but it was confined to streams running on the other side of the hills, so this particular one was quite safe. We spent many happy hours there in the open air and far from any contamination. Television had still not come to South Africa, although we heard of its wonders in the UK, but looking back, I am glad of it, as the children grew up enjoying the countryside and playing games with their friends. The dry winter months with their crisp temperatures were a perfect backdrop for many happy hours.

14

Although I celebrated my 35th birthday on 15 July 1965, I have no memory of doing so. Presumably there were birthday cards but if there were gifts, the memory has been erased. Certainly there was no card from my mother-in-law although we had sent her one twelve days earlier on 3 July.

Paul had gone to stay over with a friend of his who lived near to where we had lived in Linden and on the morning of the 17th, Ron said he did not feel too well so would go to visit his doctor and would take one of the men to drive the combi. A little later I heard the combi return and drive into the yard at the back of the quarters and the man who had taken Ron to the doctor rushed in through the back door shouting that the captain was unwell and needed help to get into the house. I raced out to find Ron slumped in the passenger seat, his face cold and sweating and the colour of putty. Between us we helped him down and into the bedroom where we laid him on the bed. I phoned for an ambulance then phoned the doctor and Margery and Bram. Otherwise there was little I could do. He told me that he was in terrible pain and murmured, 'Oh Pat, I am so ill.' Even his earlobes were a strange yellow colour as I cradled him and assured him I had sent for the ambulance. He said he had begun to feel the pain while he was at the doctor's who had wanted him to go straight to the hospital, but he had refused as he knew he was very ill and did not want to be admitted to a general ward.

As Margery and Bram arrived Ron's eyes turned up in his head and he fell back upon the bed. I tried desperately to pump his chest to no avail and as I did so the ambulance arrived and they placed him on a stretcher. As I stood at the kerbside watching, they loaded him into the ambulance, but I knew that he was dead. Margery said, 'You are going to have to be brave, Pat.'

The doctor arrived and searched in vain in his bag for something to give me for the shock. I realised I would have to call and bring Paul home, I had no idea exactly where Anne and Christopher were except that they were somewhere in the building and Cathleen was with Toni, and so I phoned, telling them what had happened but asking them not to tell Paul. Soon afterwards, his friend's parents brought him back and I took him into his bedroom and broke the news to him. After that, events are a blur. I remember some days later going with some of the family to choose Ron's coffin while I was assured that I need not worry about the cost as it had been discussed and decided that his parents, his two sisters and his brother would each pay a quarter. This was a big consideration as we had no money ourselves. The Army had been told, of course, and the commissioner and the chief secretary came to visit and give what comfort they could. The day came when we all went to the funeral parlour to see him in his coffin dressed in his Army uniform. It didn't look like him but like some waxwork model. I almost broke down at that point.

A programme was needed for the funeral service and hymns and readings had to be chosen. Margery was very insistent on ones that she thought suitable, but I ignored her and chose the ones I knew Ron had loved, especially those written by a former general of the Salvation Army, General Albert Osborne. I chose as a Bible reading Matthew chapter 25, verses 31 to 40 in which Jesus speaks of the Final Judgement and the reward for those who fed the hungry, clothed the naked and visited the prisoners, all those things which Ron had done. I had to arrange these with the printer

210

and pay for them out of my meagre resources. News had spread across the country and I was inundated with cards, telegrams and flowers. Cassie and Motie were among the first to arrive at my front door and with fixed smiles on their faces they gave me tins of cakes to use for the many visitors they knew I would have.

The day finally arrived for the funeral and it was with a stunned feeling of disbelief that I sat in the crowded hall as tributes were made to Ron and his life. The small headquarters' singing group sang the piece I had chosen, 'To the Hills', and at last we followed his coffin out into the winter sunshine where a motorcycle escort led the huge cortège to the Braamfontein Crematorium where the Army band led the procession followed by the family and all the headquarters' staff. At the back sat many of the men from the hostel. I felt frozen with grief as the coffin slid behind the curtains and I saw the last of my other half disappear for ever.

Outside the crematorium our friend Val stood and I went to speak to him. He said Cynthia had been unable to come as she was very ill in hospital; in fact, he had been unable to break the news to her as she had undergone a big operation for adhesions in her abdomen. People gathered around to give me their condolences, but it seemed quite unreal and as though it was happening to someone else.

We finally made our way back to our quarters, where we gathered for a meal. My mother-in-law was, of course, upset, and said, 'How could it happen, and just after my birthday as well?' and then added, almost unforgivably, 'Oh yes, it was just after your birthday as well, wasn't it?' So she had always known when my birthday was but had chosen to ignore it. How petty, one may think, to remember such a small thing after all these years, but hurt can take many forms. It was about this time that I realised that he had died almost five years to the day since he had received God's promise after his first heart attack.

211

Of course the children and I could no longer stay at the men's hostel and my father-in-law helped me to begin to pack up my small store of personal items before they left to return to Durban where they were living then. A few days later my brother-in-law, Ronnie, took me to one side and gave me the money from Tom and Iris, Bram and Margery and himself, but apologetically said my mother-in-law had only given half of what she had promised. I took the money down to the funeral directors and explained that I hadn't got it all, but said I would be selling some of Ron's clothes and other belongings and would bring them the rest as and when I could. Without any hesitation they said that the debt was cleared and that I had no need to raise the remainder of the money. I eventually managed to sell the combi back to the garage from which it had been bought and opened a savings account into which I put the money.

Still in shock, I waited to hear what the Army would do with me and the children. I realised it must be a problem for them but, unknown to me, there were other things going on behind the scenes. The commissioner, Commissioner Wooton, was a widower and it seemed that he had plans of his own which fitted in well with this unexpected emergency. For years the secretary to the commissioner had been a tall, middle-aged Canadian with buck teeth called Major Tuck who shared quarters with an equally unattractive friend, Captain Russell, also working at headquarters, both lovely ladies who did their jobs well. However, the commissioner was attracted to another single officer and he wanted her to be his secretary. They were to marry later on. The girls' home at Strathyre needed a new matron and so, as she had seniority to me, the secretary, who was a major, was appointed matron with her friend as assistant to live on the premises at the girls' home. I was to be quartered with my children in a small house at the back of the home. In my interview with Hesketh King, the social secretary, he said that, although

I did not have the title of matron, they would be depending on me to run things as I was the one with the experience in social work, the other two never having run a social institution before. I took up the appointment on 19 August. It was a recipe for disaster.

The home housed about 50 girls ranging in age from 5 to 16 years, most coming from broken homes. They took one look at the new matron and proceeded to run rings around her. My work started at 5.30 in the morning after leaving my own family to be looked after by my faithful Toni. I would cross to the main building and start the kitchen staff on with the breakfasts before going to wake the girls and supervise their preparations for school. Once in hand, I left the other two to continue while I went back to the kitchens to prepare the school lunches that each girl took to school with her. Once they had gone, there was the clearing up to do and then, as I was the only driver on the premises, there were groceries and vegetables to collect and children to be taken to various clinics. As if all this was not enough, hardly a night went by but I would be woken by the phone from the main building to be told that one or other of the girls had absconded. I would have to get the combi out and go to wherever they had been picked up, sometimes a police station and, on one occasion, to the local convent. I had no time for my own children, nor could I grieve for my darling husband. Additionally, Tuck and Russell would be found in tears in the matron's office.

It began to be noticed that I was losing weight and I was questioned on my eating habits. Eventually, the two hapless spinsters were pulled out and a married couple put in their place, but by then I was close to a nervous breakdown and, recognising this, I was transferred and put in charge of the young women's hostel in Kerk Street in the centre of town on 24 October 1965.

Before her father's death, Cathleen had begun to say small

words such as 'Mama' and 'Dada' and was walking and developing well. But in our altered circumstances, as well as losing her father, she virtually lost me as well, and in addition, I had no time to spend with the children, or really to have the ability to see them through their own grief. Life was a matter of existing from one day to the next, while inside I felt as though I had been torn apart. Life at the young women's hostel was an improvement, although previously it had been very well run by another female couple of majors in an efficient manner. It seemed that the same standard was expected of me although on my own and also having the responsibility of my four children. But compared with the girls' home, it was heaven.

The hostel buildings were quite old in Johannesburg terms, about 60 or 80 years old I expect, and it was already in the planning stage that the hostel was to be sold, along with the headquarters' building on Commissioner Street containing the Johannesburg City Corps' premises. A new building, combining headquarters, a new hall and a new young women's hostel, was to be built at the north end of Rissik Street and I was assured that I would take charge of the new hostel.

The hostel held about 80 young women, many of whom were Portuguese girls from Lorenzo Marques in Mozambique attending further education in the city. For their parents this was a reasonably priced and secure environment and we never had any trouble with them. Other residents were anything but 'young' but we had no age barrier, although for much older women there was a women's rest home. It was my job to oversee the staff, do the accounts, plan the menus and do the ordering. There was a big laundry on the ground floor where the sheets, towels and tablecloths were laundered every week by four 'girls' and where I held a short prayer meeting every morning. The kitchen staff included a cook and two assistants and then there were three cleaners, one for each floor, while one of the kitchen staff cleaned the

214

dining room, residents' lounge and offices on the ground floor. I had two middle-aged white ladies who did running repairs on the linen when required and who manned the office in the evenings.

Every Monday I would go to the huge linen cupboard with a note of how much fresh linen was needed after the beds had been stripped, all the sheets and so on accounted for and bundled up down into the laundry. The cupboard was a long narrow room with packed shelves on both sides and I would walk to the end and count out a pile of sheets, then turning around with my arms loaded down, I would discover behind me Cathleen and, behind her, Simba. With great difficulty I would persuade them both to back out so that I could exit with my burden!

Each week I calculated the wages, which was relatively simple as no one earned enough to pay taxes so there was no bureaucracy. Apart from the rates and major repairs, we were pretty self-sufficient and I would bank our takings and draw the money for the wages, pay the food bills by cheque and render my monthly accounts, suitably broken down, to headquarters.

Our first Christmas without Ron came around and I did my best to make it as good as possible for the children, but it was hard going. On New Year's Day we went with the rest of the Corps to Magaliesberg where we had spent such a wonderful week together. Tears were never very far away but there was no way I could give in to them as so much, and so many, depended on me. Instead I continued to lose weight and a passport photo taken at that time shows me looking haggard with dark circles under my eyes.

The passport photo was necessary as my aunts in England had asked me to come back to the UK for a visit, for which they would pay. I asked for permission to go for the six weeks prior to Cathleen's second birthday when her fare would be a mere 10 percent of the adult fare. Anne, Paul and Christopher would be suitably cared for and a retired officer would stand in for me.

So in mid-March of 1966, accompanied by many well-wishers, I arrived at Jan Smuts Airport to catch the BOAC VC10 to London. I had never flown before and will never forget that first experience of seeing the ground gradually disappear below the plane. I had a good window seat and Cathleen and I settled down to enjoy the flight. In the toilets there were bottles of expensive 'Blue Grass' hand lotions and the stewardesses were most attentive.

We were to stop at Nairobi to pick up more passengers and as we circled round I could see the airport clearly laid out below us. Suddenly the plane lifted up again and began to circle around once more. After some time we began to approach the runway again, and as I looked out of my window I saw fire engines and ambulances racing alongside the descending plane. My heart was pounding as we gradually drew to a halt and men jumped out of their trucks and ran underneath the plane. The stewardess must have seen how white and shocked I was, because she came over and told me what had happened. Apparently when the pilot put down the landing gear, his controls indicated that the front wheel had not responded. So they had circled round so that the ground crew could make a visible check to see if it was down. Apparently it seemed to be, but they had no way of knowing if it was locked into place, and so the landing was made with all the emergency vehicles on stand-by.

I don't think I would have minded if I had gone to join Ron there and then, but I was aware of the children left behind in Johannesburg ... who would have cared for them? For years afterwards, landing and taking off in an aeroplane brought me out in a cold sweat. Soon we took off again and after a brief call into Rome, where again we stayed on the plane, we were soon flying over the snow-capped Alps, eventually landing at Heathrow. I had to change planes here

216

and was impressed to be called by name and settled into my seat ahead of the other passengers because of having Cathleen with me. At last we were flying over the Tyne valley on a clear early spring day and I could see the beautiful countryside where I had grown up.

The new airport was in the process of being built at that time, and so we landed at the old airfield which Uncle Harry used to frequent, a succession of wooden huts on a windy hillside. There were crowds of the family there to greet me, as well as my old school friend Stella and her husband; it was overwhelming.

I had left Johannesburg on Saturday evening and now, here I was, sitting in Woodburn having Sunday lunch. Quite incredible. Later, Auntie Ethel pointed out an article in the Sunday papers with a story about Johannesburg and I had my first taste of media spin. The day before I had been out and about in the city doing the last-minute money changing and bits of shopping. There had been a spate of thieving in the town centre and the police were out in force looking for these snatch-and-run villains, but otherwise the town was quite calm. Now I read – and I recall the words vividly even after so many years – 'As I sit on the stoep of my hotel in Johannesburg, the air is acrid and blue with gun smoke...' It sounded like something out of the OK Corral, but certainly bore no relation to the city I had just left.

It felt quite strange to be in the house where I had spent so many of my formative years, and walking along the once-familiar city streets was the most strange sensation. It was as though I was walking through a film set; there, and yet not quite real. Much had changed of course and there was a brand-new town hall and council offices in the Haymarket. My mother's two sisters, Elsie and May, hadn't changed very much. May's husband Alfie had died and she had sold their flat and bought a little bungalow just off the coast road. They were all thrilled with Cathleen and made much of her.

It was while I was there that I began to write a piece which I subsequently entitled 'A Time to Mourn', which was later published in the South African *War Cry* and which went a long way to releasing the pent-up feelings that I had.

The six weeks passed quickly, but it gave me time to assess the situation and to realise that I would not find it too difficult to return with the children and live in England again. And so I returned to Johannesburg to catch up with all that had happened while I was away, including, I later discovered, the fact that Paul had broken his wrist and had personally removed the plaster of Paris just prior to my return. Once back, I was invited to join the Johannesburg Songsters and attended the practices every week and sang at both the Sunday services. In addition, Norman Lang, the songster leader, arranged a series of concerts at various venues up and down the Reef. I was asked to be songster sergeant, which involved doing a reading and prayers for every meeting and having the responsibility of the spiritual welfare of all the singers.

Soon the headquarters' buildings were demolished and the Sunday services were transferred to the hall in the YMCA opposite where our new hall was being built. A shop was rented on the corner of Commissioner Street just opposite the old building where Bram and Marge were in charge of Trade, and the Home League, the weekly ladies' meeting, came and used our residents' lounge, usually empty during the day. Our quarters were on the first floor and the door to it was at the head of a steep flight of uncarpeted stairs with steel treads on each step. The children and I were used to making sure that Cathleen was out of the way when we went in and out in case she fell, but one day I was at the foot of the stairs and I heard the quarters' door open and my nephew Stephen came out. To my horror, Cathleen was right behind him. I called to him to watch her, but he was confused and did not realise the danger, and as I watched helplessly, she came from behind him, stepped out and fell the full length of the stairs with Toni rushing after her. I held my breath as I rushed to the crumpled heap at the foot of the stairs, but I was soon reassured by the roars of fright which issued from her. We carefully examined her where she lay, and miraculously she was unhurt except for a few bruises.

Soon it was a year since Ron had died. Life was moving on, seeming to take me further away from him. I had also noticed that I still had that strange feeling from time to time that I had experienced on the road to Muldersvlei when we were in the Cape. I began to recognize it and as the advert would start to run in my head, I would wait for the crawling sense of fear in my gut and then the feeling of faintness. I had no idea what it was but I knew I needed to have it checked. There was a doctor in Parktown who would treat Army officers free of charge, but permission had to be obtained from headquarters. I asked Hesketh King and he gave permission and made me an appointment, but his feeling was that it was just something to do with the stress of losing Ron, although I told him I had experienced it first before Ron died.

The doctor checked me over and spent a lot of time examining my eyeballs and finally said that he thought I should be referred to the Neurological Hospital. After another examination by a consultant I was admitted to the hospital for tests. I was to be given an air encephalogram in which air would be introduced into my spinal cord which would then rise to my brain and X-rays would then be taken to see if any abnormal growth could be seen. I realised, of course, that they were thinking of a brain tumour. On the day of the test, I sat on the edge of the trolley in the X-ray room, and as my back was bent over, some spinal fluid was extracted and then the air introduced. I could feel it make its way up my back and then land like a ton of bricks onto my brain and at the same time, the 'advert' seemed to fast

219

forward while voices shouted out a loud babble of noise in my head and then I collapsed. I heard the panic in the radiologists' voices as they swung me round and quickly took the X-rays and then I was back in my bed. For two days, while the air was gradually absorbed into my system, I could not move my head. It was as if a huge piece of metal was in there against which my brain bumped whenever I moved. A few days later I was discharged with some tablets to take and an appointment to come back and see the consultant at a later date at which time, no doubt, I would be told what, if anything, they had found.

That night I took the first lot of tablets and went to bed, but later I woke up feeling desperately ill. I tried to walk but it seemed that when I lifted up my foot to step forward, my knee shot up in the air. I knew I had to get help, so woke the children and between us we managed to call an ambulance. It drove me through the deserted streets with its red light flashing and I was deposited at the casualty department of the General Hospital. I lay behind the curtains and a doctor came to examine me. I told him what had happened but he didn't seem to know what to do. Everything seemed dark, although I was not surprised as I thought they just kept the lights low at night. Suddenly I felt the need to vomit and a bowl was brought. As I finished, it was as though all the lights had come on, so I knew that whatever the tablets had done to me, I had managed to get rid of them. I was put into a bed on one of the wards and the next morning managed to contact Margery to bring me home. There I threw out all the tablets and from that day to this I have no idea what they were, but I knew they had nearly killed me. As a postscript, I attended the outpatients' department on the appointed day, but they had been unable to find my notes, so all the consultant could do was shrug his shoulders and suggest I make another appointment. But as my symptoms didn't return, I never went back. I have my own theory, which went back to the blow on my head when we lived in Bez Valley and the car went over a large bump, throwing me up against the roof. I thought it may have caused some adhesions which were removed by the air encephalogram when I heard the jumble of sensations in my head. Certainly I never had any further trouble.

The quarters were on the first floor of the building, as mentioned, at the head of a steep staircase. The front door led into a passage, with the kitchen straight ahead, although this was only used for breakfasts as we ate with the girls in the dining room downstairs. To the left at the rear of the building there were two bedrooms and the bathroom, while to the right, beyond the kitchen, was the lounge and leading directly from it, the doors to two bedrooms, the left-hand one used for Cathleen, and the right-hand one for me. Their windows looked out onto Kerk Street where, across the way, was a multi-storey car park. Below the windows was the top of an awning that shaded the pavement below. It was the height of summer and very hot, and although the evenings should have been cooler, the heat absorbed through the day by the tarmac on the streets tended to be released into the air so that there was very little respite. Consequently, I slept with the sash windows raised as far as they would go. My bed stood parallel to the double windows, and one night something woke me as I slept with my back to the window. I opened my eyes and in the oblong of light thrown in from the street lighting, I was aware of a figure crouched and moving in the window frame. Without a second's thought I leapt out of bed and pushed him out as he crouched on the sill. He fell onto the awning then picked himself up and ran to the end and down the drain pipe where he had gained access, as I watched with my head stuck out of the window and shouting at him as he went. Then I slammed both windows shut and could hardly find the strength to stagger back to my bed as the adrenalin drained out of me. Where,

I wondered, was my enormous dog, and where were all the people who must surely have heard the noise? But nothing stirred and no one heard a thing. I could have been murdered in my bed and not a soul would have noticed!

Next day, I made haste to headquarters to report on what had happened and the same day they sent someone around to put burglar bars on my bedroom windows.

Meanwhile, I was taking a correspondence course from the Army in London. The Army had a strange way of designating rank when it came to married couples. Ron had been promoted to captain, while when I was commissioned after my training, I was entitled to the rank of lieutenant. However, because I was married to a captain, my rank was Mrs Captain, but if I attained the rank for myself, I would become Captain Mrs, so to this end, instead of waiting for the powers that be to confer a rank, I could take this correspondence course and fast-track it. I badly wanted to prove myself and so undertook the studying, going on my day off across the road to the library where there was a quiet reference room in which I could study and write my essays. So in the course of time I achieved what I had set out to do and became Captain Mrs Malone.

I was constantly aware of how good God was to me. On one memorable occasion I had it in my mind to make a little white dress for Cathleen and I envisaged it in broderie anglaise. Admittedly this was a bit expensive but I thought if I saved up and shopped carefully I could find a piece sufficient for my needs. I had said nothing to anyone about this, but one evening there was a knock at the door of the quarters and one of our older residents stood there with a parcel in her hands. 'Matron,' she said, 'I've been clearing out my room and wondered if you might be able to use this?' I thanked her and when I opened it, there was a piece of broderie anglaise just sufficient for a little dress for Cathleen. I made it using a piece of an old sheet as a lining and I never forgot how God knows what we need before we even ask Him.

Time was passing and the hostel was due to close at the beginning of November so I began to give the residents plenty of notice so that they could find other accommodation. The previous officers had spent a lot of their surplus monies on buying linen for the new hostel, so I set about packing it as it was to be stored out at the Fred Clark College where the Africans were trained – a bad choice, as before the new hostel opened, the store room was broken into and all the linen stolen. As the rooms emptied I arranged for the furnishings to be bought by second-hand dealers.

Meanwhile I had had my piece, 'A Time to Mourn' published, as well as several other articles from time to time, and I was asked to be the *War Cry* reporter of the Thursday Holiness meeting and any other special meetings of interest.

It had been understood that I would be in charge of the new premises and to that end I had been involved in the choosing of kitchen equipment and a colour scheme for the rooms. But then I began to smell a rat. There was a new commissioner, Commissioner Carl Richards, and his French and forceful wife soon made plain who her favourites were, and it seemed that I was not one of them. It started off by being suggested that as I had two young sons I might not be suitable for such an appointment, although it had not troubled them when putting me into the old premises. And then I was asked to come in and see the social secretary, who told me that it had been decided that a married couple would be best able to deal with the new hostel and that I was to be appointed as side officer at the Training College, 'where my talents could best be used'.

I was stunned, but could do nothing so on 4 November 1966 we closed the doors on the old building and took the quarters' furnishings with us as we were to be housed in the flat above the laundry at the back of the college. I was

223

also told that I would have the use of a downstairs room with access only to the yard, but when we arrived, Brigadier Havercroft, the current training principal, was already loading all his books into it to use as a study, although he had a perfectly good one in the main building, but as usual I kept quiet. Toni moved with us and had a room just below us next to the one the college cook, Bella, occupied. Sadly Simba, our faithful and dearly loved companion, had suffered a growth in his abdomen and had been put to sleep. We all missed him and certainly never forgot him.

The quarters were reached up a narrow staircase which the removal men had great trouble negotiating with the wardrobes and cupboards we had brought. At the top of the stairs was a landing which took one of the wardrobes. After squeezing past it there was a bedroom for the two boys facing to the back of the building. Next to it was another bedroom for Anne and Cathleen, while the continuation of the landing provided space for our refrigerator and a small tabletop cooker. These rooms took up half the space of the flat, while the other half consisted of one large room which I divided into separate areas. Around to the right was the kitchen area with a table, a sink and a small cupboard. On the far side were a table and chairs against a window and under the other window, my bed and bedside table and alongside it the easy chairs we had brought. Although I did not have my own bedroom, I was quite happy with the arrangement. I had brought the fitted bedspreads and matching curtains from Kerk Street and it all looked very nice. With all the windows open it was possible to create a pleasant cross current if there was a bit of a breeze.

We soon settled in and I was given the task of teaching the Bible and Orders and Regulations as well as helping with the catering and the general running of the place. Toni kept our quarters clean, did the laundry and looked after Cathleen. I became a bit suspicious when Cathleen went off her food, although otherwise was quite healthy, and on questioning Toni I discovered that she had been buying her sweets when she took her to the park to gossip with all the other nannies. When a piece of fruit was substituted, she soon went back to her previous good appetite.

But although I enjoyed the work, I no longer trusted the Army to look after my interests and those of my children, and thought that I would have to make very careful plans to ultimately return to England. To that end I wrote to the Department of Health and Social Security whose central office was based in Newcastle to ask them if I could begin to pay into the National Health Scheme with a view to returning to the UK due to the death of my husband. I shall never forget the reply I received; although afterwards I realised it was a standard letter, it began with condolences at the death of my husband. It felt like a hand reached out to me at a time when I felt hemmed in on every side. They asked for a variety of certificates – birth, marriage and death – and details of where we had both worked prior to leaving the UK. I sent off as much as I could and soon I was sent some claim forms which I completed and sent back, and then put it all to the back of my mind as I had not expected that I might be entitled to anything, seeing that we had left England so many years before.

I had already booked us a holiday in Cape Town at the Army's holiday home in Fish Hoek and we were to travel there on the train from Johannesburg. The journey could be taken by spending either two nights and a day on the train, or two days and a night. We were to have a sleeper and I opted to travel two nights and a day, spending Christmas Day on the train, where we would have our Christmas dinner. We had a splendid send off from many friends and settled into our compartment where before long the attendant came to let down the beds and settle us for the night. When we woke up we were travelling through the Karoo and before long we had a long halt at Kimberley, where we were able to stretch our legs. Christopher dashed off and I was beginning to panic in case the train went without him, when he reappeared with a little brass bell that he had bought for me at one of the shops on the station. I treasure that to this very day. After our splendid Christmas lunch we dozed away the hottest parts of the day and before long we were approaching Cape Town, where the countryside changed from the harshness of the desert. We changed trains then for the local one to Fish Hoek which soon left the city and meandered along the coast so that we could appreciate the lovely vistas. It was a short walk from Fish Hoek station to the holiday home, a sprawling single-storey building where we had rooms at the back. Tired after our long journey, we settled in and had a good night's sleep, but of course everyone was awake early the next morning raring to get down to the beach. We were to be there for three weeks and I had done a deal with the older children. I would do all I could to give them a good holiday and we would have some days out, if for one day each week, they would look after Cathleen and leave me free to book three separate trips by bus to various places around the Cape which would be of no interest to them. And so it was and it worked well. I took one trip to Cape Point at the Cape of Good Hope, another around the vineyards and one to the Castle and Groot Constantia, but I drew the line at going up Table Mountain in the cable car as I wasn't very happy with heights on my own. All of us visited Muizenberg and one of the officers and his wife who were also staying there took us to the Kirstenbosch Botanical Gardens in his combi and for a spectacular drive along Chapman's Peak. But mostly we enjoyed the beach and the lovely warm sea.

All too soon it was time to catch the train back to Johannesburg and as we went along the coast on the local train once more, I told the children to take a good look at the scenery as we did not know if we would ever see it again. My mind was made up that when the time was right, I would return to England. Paul however, with the confidence of youth, declared that HE would soon be back, as I think he had dreams of becoming a rich pop star.

Some six months after I had sent off the claim forms to England, a letter finally arrived with a money order paying me a year's widow's benefit. The money was at a reduced weekly rate due to Ron not having paid anything since leaving England and I only got money for myself and nothing for the children because they were not resident in the UK. I immediately put the money into the savings account, somewhat depleted after our holiday, and from then on, when I received the postal drafts each month, I deposited them in order to save up for our return to England. Our income was pretty basic and it is difficult to put it into the context of other people's earnings at that time. Decimalisation had come in a few years previously; up to then we had been on a par with sterling pound for pound. The new notes were based on the 10-shilling note as one Rand, made up of 100 cents which was quite easy to adjust to as 5 shillings became 50 cents. Later, after our return to England when we also became decimalised, I could hardly believe the stupidity of hanging onto the pound making it 100 pence, which of course produced wild inflation, whereas in Africa, with its hugely uneducated native population, it went off without any trouble at all.

By the time we went to the Training College, I had attained my Captaincy in my own right and a copy of my Allowance Details, dated October 1966 show that for myself I received R4.03 per week with a cost-of-living bonus of R5.40. For Cathleen as a child under 5 years I received R1.00 and R2.00 each for the other children, a grand total of R16.43 a week, or R71.20 per month. Out of that we paid back for our keep R3.35 a week for me, 60 cents for Cathleen and R1.00 each for the other three. Thus it cost nothing for rent, electricity or food, and what I had left was for clothing and any incidentals I needed for the children. People were very good though, and one day I received a huge parcel from the Home League people in the Eastern Cape containing many lengths of material suitable for making dresses and shirts, and a huge box of biscuits. Once more, God had been very good to us and I was able to make many things with the material.

The Havercrofts moved on and Colonel and Mrs George King took over as Principals. The Kings had one son, George who was a year or two older than my children. He had been very strictly brought up by his parents with his nose kept to the grindstone and every minute of his day was set out for him. My lot were a revelation to him and they all spent many happy hours in the garden together. This, however, didn't suit the Colonel. When Christopher came home from school he was told that he must use the back gate, but he couldn't reach over the top to unbolt it, and so would continue to come to the front. The Colonel found this difficult to accept and expected my children to remain unseen. However, when the time came to take the Cadets on campaign, he insisted that I accompany them, leaving the older ones with Toni and taking Cathleen with us. As she was barely three, this was no joke as we travelled by combi to the Eastern Cape once more, and on one memorable occasion as I was preaching, behind the dais Cathleen clung to my leg and refused to be moved. At one of the quarters we stayed at I was expected to go with them to the native location to do Sunday School work in the afternoon with the Cadets. The Corps Officer's wife must have seen how exhausted I was and prevailed upon the Colonel to leave Cathleen and I behind, where I gratefully sank into bed with Cathleen flat out beside me.

I had continued to write for the *War Cry* and at one point Commissioner Richards asked if I could accompany him around on his tours of the country to report on the meetings he held, but of course that was out of the question. Meanwhile, however, I discovered a talent for writing poems, some of which seemed to come from my continuing grief. I have forgotten most of them and lost the clippings from the *War Cry* that I had kept for some time, but one remains that was written shortly after Cathleen turned three years old and was called 'The Gift':

Relaxed upon my knee she sleeps,
Her closed lids hiding hazel eyes
So often widened in surprise
At all around her which she sees,
The birds, the flowers, the moving trees,
And gold fish flashing in the pool...

Today the others went to school,
And so we two in company,
Sat down to have our morning tea.
And then, because she's just turned three,
She sought the comfort of my knee.

I bend my head to silken hair,
With red-gold tints, not dark nor fair,
And curled up close against my wrist
Is one small, dimpled, plump warm fist.

Her breathing rises soft and slow,
And as the world goes to and fro,
I treasure up these moments rare,
And offer up a silent prayer,
For this sweet unexpected child,
Whose nature is so warm and mild.

Oh Lord I pray, that even as the gift was given,
I may return it to our God in Heaven.

This was also published, but as I don't have a copy; this is written here from memory and may not be completely accurate.

I was becoming to feel more and more hedged in and under constant criticism, but events were to move on and bring me to a final decision about my family's future.

15

As songster sergeant, I had the spiritual care of the songster members, and one couple was a cause for great concern. The young people had not been married for very long but were experiencing a lot of trouble in settling down together. The Corps officer, a captain who in later years would become Commissioner for South Africa, was in the habit of giving me a lift back to the college after the weekly practice, and such was our concern that we would sit and talk for some time about the problems these young people were having. Unknown to either of us, however, curious eyes were peeping out of the windows and commenting on this perfectly innocent conversation. Before long, Mrs King took to me one side and, to my astonishment, spoke to me about this so-called liaison. I put her mind at rest in no uncertain terms but she seemed unconvinced.

At the local Fairview Corps there was a man known as Brother Ferreira who had great influence on the doings there although I have no idea what his qualifications may have been. It was announced, however, that he would be coming to the college to give a talk to the cadets and that I was expected to attend. So I found myself sitting there listening to a lecture about good behaviour on the part of an Army officer and making sure that actions could not be misconstrued. The cadets may have been somewhat bemused by this lecture, but I knew without a shadow of a doubt that it was aimed directly at me. I was incensed. Had I been about to conduct an affair with this captain, I most certainly would not have done it in a car parked directly in front of the training college and in full view of anyone who cared to look. I never mentioned this to the captain as I felt he would have been embarrassed to think that his actions had provoked such a reaction and, needless to say, the Kings never went so far as to speak to *him* as I was the easier target. If I had had any doubts about returning to England, this settled things for me.

I told Mrs King what my intentions were. She was horrified and warned me not to take myself away from the Army's care, but I had every confidence that I could provide for my family as I had already had many years of working at a variety of jobs before we became Army officers.

The political situation in the country was becoming very intense. Where previously the police and other authorities had kept their activities quiet, newspaper articles were beginning to appear criticising the pass system and reporting on some of the arrests that were being made. There was a tense atmosphere in the townships, but on one occasion I remember, I was able to join a group on a visit to Soweto. Europeans (as all white people were called, wherever they may have hailed from) had to obtain special permission to enter any of the townships. I don't recall what the occasion was but I was fascinated by the long straight roads lined with small brick-built houses each with a fruit tree planted in the front garden. We were made welcome by the lady of the house and seated in her small front room, where tea was served to us and we were able to sit and chat. Afterwards we all went to a big meeting for the black Salvationists as, under apartheid, worshipping was a separate thing. The hall was packed, the noise was deafening and each speaker was greeted with loud cheers. As the meeting reached its climax the people leaped up and paraded up and down the aisles with shouts and ululations, praising the Lord in no uncertain terms. What an experience, and one I would not have missed for anything.

Meanwhile, the children were growing up. Anne was 16 and was turning into a lovely young girl. She had attracted the attention of a young man called Rainie Strydom who was in his 20s and who had recently completed his compulsory two year army training. He was often a guest in our small quarters and I could see how enamoured of my daughter he was. This was a difficult situation, because as a widow, I had to act as both father and mother to my family. So I took Rainie to one side one day and told him that I was putting him on his honour to treat my daughter with respect. He heard me out with great courtesy and told me I had no need to worry on his account. I knew that soon I would have to make a decision about our future because as the children matured, there may well be romances of a more important nature which may have prevented us from, or made it more difficult to, return to the UK.

Paul, as well as his cousin Stephen, Margery's youngest boy, was attending the John Orr Technical College, while Christopher was still struggling with his dyslexia at his junior school. Additionally I had begun to realise that Cathleen had some problems. Her talking was very slow and when asked to 'say doggy' instead of saying 'doggy' she would repeat 'say doggy'. I had never experienced this with my other children and could not help but wonder if the traumatic events of her father's death and our uprooting from one place to another had not, in some way, contributed to a disruption of her learning processes.

Another officer had been appointed to the Training College, Captain Mary Salmon. She had done a spell in South Africa before returning to the UK for family reasons, but now she had been reappointed back to South Africa and to the Training College. She and I became great friends and at last I was able to share my feelings and emotions with someone who was prepared to listen with a sympathetic ear. Before long I gradually began to feel that, at last, I was returning to something resembling a normal life. I no longer felt continually divorced from reality, but from time to time, a feeling of well-being would come upon me and I would think 'Oh yes, this is what things used to feel like before Ron died'. It was 1967, two years since his death, and at last I could start to think of moving on.

My savings were reaching the point at which I might be able to pay for airline tickets for us all. The end of the school year was approaching and I had heard of a cheap airline to the UK. Mrs Captain Neilson, who ran the home for older ladies, had a resident whose son owned the airline and she offered to speak to him on my behalf. A little while later she came to me with the news that I could have cheap tickets to fly in early January of 1968, but that we would not be able to travel all together. Two of us would have to go first and then there would be three tickets available for about a week later. I found I would be able to afford it and went to see a travel agent in town as I would have to arrange for flights from London to Newcastle. The agent wasn't sure which airport in London we would be landing at but the Newcastle flight would leave from Heathrow. I drew the money out of the savings account and paid for our tickets and then I bought some cheap suitcases for us all. A big problem was shopping for winter weight clothing at the height of a South African summer, so I trawled all the 'Sammy' shops in Troyeville and elsewhere and was able to buy an assortment of outdated clothing which would tide us over to begin with.

Our Christmas holiday was spent at the home of a family who were on vacation. This was not unusual. People were wary of leaving their homes unoccupied for any length of time as burglars were notorious for breaking in and clearing out all the contents. We heard of this home through another officer who had been approached by the family concerned. It was in the suburb of Emmerentia on the road to the Linden

234

Boys' Home and Captain Stephenson through whom we had heard of it, undertook to take us there in the Linden combi and see us settled in. It was a comfortable ranch-style home with, joy of joy, an en-suite bathroom and pleasant lawned gardens.

We settled in to enjoy our final weeks in South Africa and were able to join in all the Christmas activities at the Corps. The new building was completed and that Christmas we had some wonderful social evenings with games and lots of laughter and I arranged a leaving party for the family to which almost everyone came. We returned to the training college for our last few weeks and we all went out to the airport to see Anne and Paul off. It was a big step to send them off on their own but I had every confidence in their ability to take care of themselves, and so we watched as they skipped off towards the steps to the plane and continued watching until it took off and vanished to the north and Europe. Two weeks later, with Christopher, Cathleen and as much luggage as we could carry between us, I too made the trip to the airport and was seen off by as many of the Corps as could manage to come in the course of a working day. There were many fond farewells and promises to write and then we were through passport control into the departure lounge and waiting to be called to the plane.

It was January 1968, almost exactly fourteen years since I had had my first sight of the South African shore. The two children I had had then had already left, I was now taking with me the two children born in this land, but I was leaving behind me the man I had met and loved and who had turned my world upside down. I had no idea what the future might hold for any of us as I sat beside my children, surrounded by our few possessions and the clothes we stood up in, and with the sum of £50 waiting in the Newcastle Building Society left to me by my great-aunt.

Perhaps Mrs King was right and I should not have taken

235

myself out of the hands of the Army, but I knew I was in the hands of God and that was far more important. I had been enabled to use all my talents in the last few years and I had enjoyed some wonderful experiences, but I knew the time had come for me to return to my home ground and make a new life for us all.

The plane was ready, we walked out and boarded it, and as we flew off I took my last look at the far-flung veldt with its hazy horizons cloaked by the smoke of the township fires.